People Who Make A Difference

Delron Shirley

2009

This teaching manual is intended for personal study; however, the author encourages all students to also become teachers and to share the truths from this text with others. However, copying the text itself without permission from the author is considered plagiarism which is punishable by law. To obtain permission to quote material from this book, please contact:
Delron Shirley
3210 Cathedral Spires Dr.
Colorado Springs, CO 80904
www.teachallnationsmission.com
teachallnations@msn.com

Table of Contents

People with Purpose	1
People of Passion	6
People with a Plan	10
People in Position	13
People Who Have Pity	17
People of Purity	24
People of Prayer	29
People with Power	31
People of Perseverance	37
People Who Believe in Their Personal Witness	40
People with Paper	43
People Who are Prejudice-free	50
People of Prophecy	55
People of Piety	58
People Who Understand Prosperity	70
People of Praise	80
People with Positive Confessions	85
People Who Face Persecution	88

People with Purpose

The king squinted as his eyes rushed to adjust to the flood of light that invaded his tent when the flap was opened. His heart pumped just a bit harder from the adrenaline that was released from the anticipation that he was about to get the answer he had anxiously awaited for nearly three fortnights. At long last someone had stepped forward to accept the gargantuan challenge placed before his army. For forty days and nights, his men had run like scared rabbits scurrying for cover every time their foe had repeated his threat. Now, someone had finally decided to ante up and face the monster.

Towering nearly seven feet tall, the king was accustomed to bending down a bit to look his subjects in the eye, but today he had to arch his neck and back even more than he was accustomed to. The guest who had been ushered into his presence was not one of his burly soldiers, but a skinny little excuse for a boy. Though he was weathered by long days of exposure to the elements, this redheaded lad still bore the softness of a pampered little kid. Words of surprise erupted from the monarch's mouth, "You're just a kid! How in heaven's name do you think that you can fight against a giant?" As the boy answered, Saul gradually became convinced that there really was something about this youngster that made him deserve to be listened to. Although his opponent was a decorated warrior with a long record including almost too many victories to count and although he was a fierce warrior with an impenetrable armor girding almost every inch of his nine-foot stature, King Saul realized that Goliath really could be taken down by the little shepherd boy who stood before him on this monumental occasion.

The determination to allow David to go forward with his plan to fight against the Philistine was likely the most pivotal decision King Saul had ever made--or would ever make. His whole career and his nation's destiny hung in the balance of this one decision. The giant's challenge was that one man of Israel was to face him in a winner-take-all fight to the death. The one who emerged the victor would win freedom for his people; the one who fell in the contest would sell his nation into slavery. For the king to be willing to put his whole nation at jeopardy in the hands of a little boy who had shown up from nowhere was an unheard-of act of bravery--or foolishness--on the part of the ruler. Why was he willing to "put all his eggs in one basket," especially such an unlikely basket as a shepherd boy who said that he was going to confront the ironclad behemoth of a man with just a simple slingshot?

Perhaps the answer lies in the report that had occasioned the lad's entrance into the king's field operations tent. When David had showed up at the battleground, his whole intent was to bring a care package from his father to his three senior brothers who were enlisted in the king's battalions and to collect a little news about his brothers' wellbeing to bring back to the father upon his return. His brothers, embarrassed by their cowardice before the giant's threatening, ridiculed the boy claiming that his objective was to badmouth them when he got back home.

David's response was that he had no evil intent and then questioned their own motives with the enquiry, "Is there not a cause?" Interestingly enough, he was told on at least three occasions that King Saul had put up a generous bounty for anyone who would go up against the giant--his daughter's hand in marriage, tax-exempt status for his family, and a huge monetary reward for the warrior. Still, none of the king's men were motivated by even such a great prize awaiting their bravery. David, on the other hand, seemed unaffected by the allurement of the reward money and status afforded to the victor. For him, there was a cause that far exceeded the price tag attached to the bounty placed on Goliath's head. His concern was that the giant had defied the army of the living God. With God's reputation at stake, the little shepherd boy had a motivation that could not be found in the hearts of any of the other men gathered in the Valley of Elah that day. The love he had for the object of the psalms he had composed as he wandered about the hillsides of Bethlehem was more intense than anything that could be bought with a royal bride, tax-free living, or a bulging purse. Something more powerful burned inside his soul and spirit--something that when it was reported to the king made the ruler certain that he had found the necessary element for facing the giant's challenge. The thing that burned inside David's young heart was purpose.

Purpose transforms ordinary people into men and women who can make a difference no matter what giant looms in their way--whether it be the giant of poverty in Haiti, the giant of almost one-hundred-billion-percent inflation in Zimbabwe, the giant of AIDS in Uganda, the giant of genocide in Rwanda, the giant of tsunami waves in Sri Lanka, the giant of a military jaunta's dictatorial rule in Myanmar, the giant of a Maoist revolution in Nepal, or the giant that casts his ugly shadow across the path that leads to your personal future and well-being.

The one individual who made the greatest difference in all of human history was Jesus Christ, a man of purpose. Dr. Luke described the Master's purposeful determination in verse fifty-one of chapter nine in his biography of Jesus by saying that He had steadfastly set his face to go to Jerusalem. This passage is an allusion to the expression of having set one's face like a flint in the prophetic passage Isaiah 50:4-9 which dramatically predicts the crucifixion. In other words, Jesus had a purpose for His life--and that purpose was His sacrificial death! In fact, He specifically told us this at least twice. In the Garden of Gethsemane, as He languished over the coming agony, He refused to be moved off of His purpose saying, "For this cause came I unto this hour." (John 12:27) Then as He stood before Pilate and was offered what we would call today a plea bargain, He again stood firm on His purpose, "To this end was I born, and for this cause came I into the world." (John 18:37)

In the Apostle Paul, we see another individual of

purpose who generated a difference in his world. Numerous times he spoke of having a cause motivating his life and actions. (Romans 15:9; I Corinthians 4:17; Ephesians 3:1, 14; Colossians 1:9; I Thessalonians 2:13; Titus 1:5) When the prophet Agabus warned him of impending doom and all his friends tried to dissuade him from continuing his journey which led him headlong into prison, he refused with the argument, "What mean ye to weep and to break mine heart? for I am ready not to be bound only, but also to die at Jerusalem for the name of the Lord Jesus." (Acts 21:13) Purpose made him willing to pay any price necessary.

In the Old Testament book of Esther, we read the story of the birth of purpose in the heart of a beauty queen. When her uncle first shared with her the determined plight of the Jewish people, she dismissed the matter feeling that her position in the palace made her immune to the coming holocaust; however, when Mordecai's words eventually impregnated her spirit, purpose was conceived.

> Then Mordecai commanded to answer Esther, Think not with thyself that thou shalt escape in the king's house, more than all the Jews. For if thou altogether holdest thy peace at this time, then shall there enlargement and deliverance arise to the Jews from another place; but thou and thy father's house shall be destroyed: and who knoweth whether thou art come to the kingdom for such a time as this? Then Esther bade them return Mordecai this answer, Go, gather together all the Jews that are present in Shushan, and fast ye for me, and neither eat nor drink three days, night or day: I also and my maidens will fast likewise; and so will I go in unto the king, which is not according to the law: and if I perish, I perish. (Esther 4:13-16)

In the New Testament, we find a parallel story when we follow Peter from the Garden of Gethsemane on Maundy Thursday to the Upper Room on Pentecost. He started out running away and wound up preaching fearlessly that all his subjects were guilty before God for the death of Jesus. What had happened? He had found purpose in the resurrection. (Acts 2:24, 32; 3:15, 26; 4:10; 5:30; 10:40; I Peter 1:21) He was no longer the hireling which Jesus said in John 10:11-13 would run away when danger came; he had become the shepherd which Jesus commissioned him to be on the shore of the Galilee shortly after the resurrection (John 21:15-17, I Peter 5:1-3)--the shepherd willing to lay down his life for the sheep.

Unfortunately, much of the world--and tragically, much of the church--has yet to be awakened to the purpose that will make them into men and women who can and will make a difference. As long as the pastors of our churches have just enough members to pay their salaries, they can exist in survival mode and their congregations will not make a difference in their communities and their world. Proverbs 29:18 proclaims that the people perish where there is no vision; truly, people all around the world are perishing today because so many Christians have no vision--no purpose! If you want to make a difference in a perishing world, let God birth purpose inside you!

People of Passion

When he was just a youngster, the Lord had spoken purpose into Jeremiah's heart--he was to be a prophet to the nations. However, the job became a real "pain in the neck" to him, getting him into constant trouble and eventually landing him in prison. Eventually, he decided to just "throw in the towel," so he ripped up his business cards and stomped out into his front yard and yanked up the marquee, "Jeremiah, prophet of the Lord." However, it was only a few days until he was back at the printer ordering new cards and back in the front yard with his posthole diggers replacing the signpost. Why? He described what happened to him as if there was a fire inside his bones--a fire of such intensity that he couldn't help but let it erupt with volcanic fury. What Jeremiah was experiencing was passion: purpose with muscle--purpose on steroids, if you please.

When purpose turns to passion, it becomes a fire that burns unquenchably inside the human spirit and then, like a contagious disease, begins to affect and infect everyone around. Remember what happened with David in the Valley of Elah. Before the dust had settled from Goliath's crash to the ground, every one of the soldiers of the Israeli army grabbed his weapon and attacked the Philistine army. Although they had cowered behind the rocks and bushes for more than a month, it took only one display of purpose turned to passion to set them aflame. They rose up and pursued the enemy to the very gates of their capital cities of Ekron and Gath, littering the hillsides with the corpses of the men who once engendered debilitating terror in them. Such is the work of passion!

Passion is the drive that gives us a reason for getting out of bed each morning. <u>The Bible in Basic English</u> uses "passion" in a number of verses to communicate the concept of zeal or driving motivation.

> Through Phinehas, and because of his <u>passion</u> for my honour, my wrath has been turned away from the children of Israel, so

that I have not sent destruction on them all in my wrath. (Numbers 25:11)

Then the king sent for the Gibeonites; (now the Gibeonites were not of the children of Israel, but were the last of the Amorites, to whom the children of Israel had given an oath; but Saul, in his <u>passion</u> for the children of Israel and Judah, had made an attempt on their lives:) (II Samuel 21:2)

I am on fire with <u>passion</u> for your house (For the zeal of thine house hath eaten me up--KJV); and the hard things which are said about you have come on me. (Psalms 69:9)

The <u>passion</u> of my soul's desire is for the house of the Lord (My soul longeth, yea, even fainteth for the courts of the LORD--KJV); my heart and my flesh are crying out for the living God. (Psalms 84:2)

And it came to the minds of the disciples that the Writings say, I am on fire with <u>passion</u> for your house. (John 2:17)

Notice the wording of Psalm 69:9 and its New Testament reference in John 2:17: "I am on fire with passion." The idea of being set ablaze with passion is reminiscent of Jeremiah's summation of how the Word of God was the driving force in his life, "Then I said, I will not make mention of him, nor speak any more in his name. But his word was in mine heart as a burning fire shut up in my bones, and I was weary with forbearing, and I could not stay." (verse 20:9) A similar thought is suggested in the story of the two men who walked with the Risen Lord on the road to Emmaus when they summed up their encounter with Him by saying, "Did not our heart burn within us, while he talked with us by the way, and while he opened to us the scriptures?" (Luke 24:32) John Wesley echoed their testimony when he chronicled a journal entry concerning his conversion to Christ on May 24, 1783:

> In the evening, I went very unwillingly to a society in Aldersgate Street, where one was reading Luther's preface to the Epistle to the Romans. About a quarter before nine, while he was describing the change which God works in the heart through faith in Christ, I felt my heart strangely warmed. I felt I did trust in Christ, Christ alone for salvation, and an assurance was given me that he had taken away my sins, even mine, and saved me from the law of sin and death.

In each of these cases, something kindled a fervent motivation for a cause or purpose in their hearts. The question is, "How does this happen and what is it that can set a person's heart ablaze with such a passion for his cause?" If we can find any consistent point in each of these examples, it would be the Word of God. For Jeremiah, it was the internalized Word; for the disciples on the road, it was the preached Word; for Wesley, it was the written Word. Certainly Phinehas, King Saul, and the Psalmist also shared this one common factor of the Word of God as a kindling force for passion in their lives. Phinehas, as the grandson of the high priest Aaron and the great nephew of the lawgiver Moses, had been raised in an environment saturated with the Word of God. Saul, as the king of Israel, had handwritten a personal copy of the Torah as his own personal guidebook for life. (Deuteronomy 17:18) David had not only studied the Word for his own correction and instruction (Psalm 119:11), he also authored a major portion of the book of Psalms. Passion is kindled by God's Word--either the written Word on the pages of holy scripture or the individually breathed Word in our hearts.

It was already dark when Mrs. O'Leary headed out to the barn to milk Ole Bessie on the evening of October 8, 1871, so she grabbed her lantern as she headed for her task.[1] Before long Mrs. O'Leary was smiling over her half-filled pale, but for some reason Ole Bessie didn't seem as pleased as did the milk maid. Suddenly, the cow bolted a bit and landed a kick square into the lantern, sending it tumbling into the straw scattered about on the barn floor. Instantly, the barn burst into an uncontrollable inferno which raced like an Olympic sprinter to the farm house and then the neighbor's home and then the home next to it. By the time the raging flames were squelched two days later, thirty-four blocks of the city of Chicago lay in ashes and embers. Mrs. O'Leary and Ole Bessie certainly made a difference; however, it was not a positive difference. Their escapade was a testimony to the contagious power of the flames of passion, and at the same time, an indictment against the destructive power of passion out of control. Passion without direction can be as destructive as a fire without a furnace. That's why those men and women who are to make a positive difference must be sure that they are also people with the next unavoidable quality--a plan.

---

[1] Yes, I know that this only an urban legend, but it does add some color to the narrative.

People with a Plan

"But you see, sir, here's the deal. If you tax the people too heavily, they'll revolt or possibly just become too discouraged to be productive since they are only allowed to keep such a small percentage of the production. Either way, you lose. Certainly the math works out that you should impose a fifty-percent tariff, but you see it's psychology--not mathematics--that you have to consider. You have to calculate the highest percentage that you can take without stirring up the people. If you collect twenty percent but are careful with how you store it so that the rats don't eat it all up, and if you properly manage it, you should have a sufficient supply to get everybody through the tough times. We both know human nature well enough to know that the people are not going to save anything on their own; so when the famine hits, the only way they are going to feed their families is to buy their own grain back from you. If you work the plan properly, you'll own everything--the livestock, the fields, and even the people as indentured servants--by the time the famine is over!"

Although Joseph was fresh out of prison and had nothing on his previous resume' except slavery, the king of the country turned a keen ear to his counsel and immediately offered him the position directly under his own. Why? It was simple; Joseph had a plan. Just as King Saul had seen into the little shepherd boy's heart and determined that he had what it takes to be a man who makes a difference--purpose, Pharaoh could see into this prisoner's mind and had found that he had the next vital ingredient to becoming a man who makes a difference--a plan.

Putting a plan to one's purpose and passion is a universal requirement in making a difference in one's world. The instant Esther realized that there was a cause for her being in the royal entourage, she developed a plan for fulfilling that purpose. She declared a time of fasting followed by her appeal before Ahasuerus in which she invited the king and Haman to the first in a series of two lavish banquets. Knowing that the way to a man's heart is through his stomach, she didn't want to fail by only getting a halfhearted response to her request. Only after she heard an irrepressible belch from the king on the follow-up feast was she confident that she had won his undivided attention. It was only then that she was willing to risk presenting her request that the Jews be allowed to defend themselves during the planned genocide on the thirteenth day of the month of Adar. Once the king's decree was made and the Jews proved victorious on the first Purim in history, she continued with her plan and won permission for the mêlée to continue one more day so that they could totally eradicate the malicious faction.

When Nehemiah added a plan to his purpose, he was able to generate passion that drew the populace of Jerusalem into action. Men who had lived amidst the rubble of the broken down wall for years rallied around Nehemiah and his plan. Within fifty-two days, the reconstructed walls rose majestically out of the debris that had disgraced the city for decades.

In 1946, a young Canadian missionary stood on a street corner in the recently surrendered Kingdom of the Rising Sun, passing out gospel tracts to the thousands who passed each day. Jack McAlister definitely had a purpose--to penetrate Japan with the gospel of Jesus Christ. However, he realized that he needed more than just one street corner and a bag of tracts to do so; he needed a better plan. So he asked the Lord to give him one. Within a few days, he was not only had a purpose, but a plan as well--and a plan that required contagious passion because it called for an army of volunteers to visit every home in Japan and leave a piece of Christian literature. Purpose, plan, and passion synergized into a program that not only penetrated the Japanese islands, but snowballed as it invaded nation after nation until, within six decades, over one and a quarter billion homes had been visited with almost three billion pieces of literature distributed, resulting in close to seventy million responses. It was having a plan that made the difference in the world through World Literature Crusade (now know as Every Home for Christ). If you are going to make a difference, you must also have a divinely inspired plan. If you don't know where you are going, you'll not know when you get there or if even if you are there if you were to ever get there. Winning the world for Christ requires more than just unlocking church door every Sunday morning and screaming loudly into your microphone with the volume turned up as high as it will go. It requires a strategic plan focused on a God-given purpose that incorporates the energy of passion.

People in Position

King Artaxerxes had a reason for paying close attention to Nehemiah's face. Nehemiah was his cupbearer, the royal food tester. Every plate of food and every cup of beverage had to pass by Nehemiah before it was offered to the king. Only after Nehemiah had sampled everything on the king's menu, was it deemed safe for the monarch's consumption. With his very life dependent upon Nehemiah's welfare, the king had learned to carefully read every expression on the cupbearer's face, watching for any indication of an ill reaction to the food or beverage he had tasted. And today he had reason for concern as there was a certain darkness about Nehemiah's countenance. Although the king could tell that his food taster was not physically ill from lethal poison, there was still cause for some alarm. As he questioned the cupbearer, the king learned that Nehemiah was emotionally distraught concerning the fate of his hometown, Jerusalem. When his cousins, who had recently visited, shared with Nehemiah how the city was in disrepair and the wall lay in ruins, he was troubled and challenged to try to remedy the situation. Purpose had been birthed, a plan was in the gestation period, and passion was soon to emerge as well; but today Nehemiah discovered the next all-important element in becoming a man who makes a difference--position.

Though he had come to Persia as a slave, God had strategically situated him in the king's court with a job that kept him constantly in the ruler's eyesight. Though the title seems impressive, it must be remembered that the whole reason for Nehemiah's job was because he was totally expendable. No one of any significance would be put in the place of facing possible poisoning on a daily basis. However, this one position was the only one that would have precipitated the conversation that would lead to Nehemiah's appointment to the task of rebuilding the walls.

God has a unique way of moving the people who are destined to make a difference into the positions they need to be in to effect the changes that they are to bring. Although he resisted going to Nineveh, Jonah wound up on the world's first submarine ride to one of the major cities in that period of history. (verses 1:2; 3:2, 3; 4:1) Jesus may have started out in the insignificant cities of Bethlehem and Nazareth, but He ended up in the capital city of Jerusalem because He knew that the platform of His ministry was tied inextricably to that one significant city. (Luke 13:33, Matthew 16:21, John 7:3-5) Who would have though that the little shepherd boy who came bearing a few care packages would ever be ushered into the king's tent? After all, his big brother Eliab who tried to laugh him off the battlefield never got invited in. What about Joseph--what are the chances that a man would walk straight out of prison into the second highest place of authority in the greatest world empire of the time? Daniel went to Babylon as a slave, but was eventually elevated to one of the principle leaders and policy makers. Even the little slave girl in Naaman's household was in a position to speak into the life of one of the great generals of the nation where she had been taken captive. The story of Esther echoes the same truth; if we can dig through the layers of lacquer and glitter that have been applied to her story though the years, we'll recognize her role in the Persian Empire for what it was--little more than the king's sex toy. Yet, it was exactly the place that she needed to be in in order to save the entire Jewish race. No one would ever have imagined that this little orphan girl, without a drop of "blue blood" in her veins, would wind up in the palace at "such a time as this"--but it happened because the Lord is able to put men and women of purpose in places of position. If a person has a purpose, God will give him a platform from which to launch his plan. Proverbs 18:16 declares that a man's gift will make a place for him and bring him before great men. Certainly purpose, passion, and plans qualify for gifts that will guarantee a God-given position.

      We must remember, however, that we will not be supernaturally parachuted into every position with no involvement of our own. We can take the life of the Apostle Paul for example. He was born in Tarsus which by his own estimation was no mean (average) city. (Acts 21:39) From the very incident of his conversion, the apostle knew that he was destined to bear witness of the faith to men in significant places; therefore, he seemed to deliberately position himself in places where his message would have the possibility of reaching the ears of noteworthy men. He insisted on being in the very jugular vein of his society. If we analyze the cities he chose for his ministry centers, we will readily see that each was a strategic location: Damascus, located on the convergence of the three major caravan routes of the ancient world and an abundant water supply, was the leading city of ancient Syria in terms of commerce and agriculture; Antioch, near the Mediterranean coast, was the third largest city in the Roman Empire and had a main street paved with marble and flanked by colonnades; Antioch in Pisidia, having been made a Roman colony by Emperor Augustus, was actually ruled by several members of the imperial household; Salamis was one of the major cities on the island of Cyprus; Phillipi was a cosmopolitan Roman colony city located on the Egnatian Way, the primary road crossing Macedonia; Thesslonica was a major port city in Macedonia, which is modern-day Greece; Athens, flourishing from sea trade from the Mediterranean world, had an air of grandeur because of the temples and other public buildings and its heritage of philosophy and Greek culture; Corinth, located on the isthmus that connects northern and southern Greece, was a transfer point for ships which didn't want to sail around the entire Greek peninsula; Ephesus a major port city on the western coast of Asia Minor, was the center for seaborne trade and the hub of the region's road system as well as an administrative center for the province of Asia and the site of renowned religious shrines, a spacious theater, stadium, and elegant public buildings; Troas, just south of the ancient city of Troy, was an important port city along the Aegean Sea; Jerusalem, the capital of ancient Israel, was the central city for Jewish life and the site of the temple; Caesarea was the principal port city and administrative center for Roman Palestine; Rome, the capital of the Roman Empire, was the largest and most important city in the ancient world. Even if he had to go bound in chains, he continually strategized to get himself into the position (Acts 25:11-12) to bear witness to the very top men in the empire (Philippians 4:22).

When Dr. Lester Sumrall was directed by God to go to the Philippines to start a work for the Lord, his denomination tried send him to a little mission outstation but he resisted and insisted that he had to be located in the capital city of Manila. The result was that his ministry there precipitated a revival in which over one hundred fifty thousand Filipinos were saved--something that could have never happened in a hidden-away corner of the country. From that great revival in the major population center, the new converts spread through the nation carrying with them the message of the gospel. In his own words, Dr. Sumrall used to express his mission strategy, "Most of world's nations have one major city. Go there and plant the gospel. As long as "Mamma" is alive, the message will reach villages."

If you are one of those who is going to make a difference, God has a place for you--and He will help you find it and, more importantly, He will help you get there!

People Who Have Pity

Although he had always made it a special point to only travel as part of a large group when he had to transverse the desolate road through this unguarded territory, for some reason which seems almost inconsequential by now he had decided to team up with these two strangers on today's journey. They had only traveled a few miles when something bizarre happened. His "friends" suddenly morphed into the fiends they really were. One suddenly brandished the most no-nonsense dagger our friend had ever seen. In a flash its sharp point was pressed hard against the thin flesh protecting his jugular vein. The other bandit grabbed our friend's bag and began to rummage through it, tossing out anything that was not of immediate cash value. Next, they ripped off our friend's clothes and tore them to shreds looking for any hidden pockets where more cash might be concealed. Then everything went dark as he felt a harsh blow against his left temple. He wasn't sure how much time actually lapsed before he began to regain consciousness, but he could tell that the sun had moved several paces in its arch across the sky as he dizzily began to recognize his surroundings. Trying hard to focus, he was able to distinguish that it was a pair of sandals that was kicking up the dust a few feet away from him. Straining his eyes even more, he could tell that the figure above that cloud of dust wore the robes of one of the temple priests. His heart leapt as he imagined that God had sent one of His men to help him. But suddenly, something unthinkable happened; that pair of feet changed their course and diverted to the opposite side of the road and disappeared! For a few seconds, our friend questioned if it had been an hallucination--but no matter how much his head was spinning, he was unquestionably certain that it had been real. Still in a semiconscious twilight zone, he saw a second set of sandals approaching him. Again, he struggled to reach up and call out to his rescuer; his spirit was crushed once more as he followed the sandals as they crossed to the far side of the road eventually disappearing out of sight. He was certain that it had not been a mirage daunting him with the illusion that this second traveler was also a man of the cloth--a Levite. After collapsing into another period of unconsciousness brought on by the loss of blood and his worsening dehydration in the unrelenting sun, our friend came to just in time to realize that another figure was nearby. This time the traveler stopped, dismounted, and bent over him. At first our friend gasped because he recognized the figure to be a Samaritan. With visions of the longstanding animosity between the two races, our friend questioned if this stranger had an even more vile intent than his two previous attackers. But suddenly, he heard comforting words and felt the refreshing wipe of a cool cloth and the invigorating sensation of a rejuvenating sip of wine. How could it be that two "men of God" had passed him by like a heap of human refuse but this stranger, whom he considered a "son of Belial," had stopped to care for him?

When Jesus told the story, He explained that the Samaritan stopped and helped because he had been moved with compassion. Even though the priest and the Levite had been put in a position to make a difference, they lacked the next significant quality necessary to be men who make a difference--pity.

The scriptures, both in the Old and New Testaments, are replete with directives to care for widows, orphans, and fatherless. The Father is painted as one who cares for the destitute so much that He considers any gift given to them as if it were placed in His own hands (Proverbs 19:17) and any service rendered to them as an action directly for the Lord (Matthew 25:40). Jesus Himself is portrayed as the high priest who is touched with the feelings of human infirmities (Hebrews 4:15). This divine quality of pity, generally labeled as "compassion," is portrayed as the basic motivating force in the life of Jesus. It was pity, or compassion, that moved Him to minister to human need on every level--body, soul, and spirit. Because of compassion,

Jesus took care of physical needs such as healing (Matthew 14:14, 20:34; Mark 1:41) and hunger (Matthew 15:32, Mark 8:2). He taught parables which portrayed the mandate of compassion or pity in such physical activities of ministering to wounded brothers (Luke 10:33) and blessing those indebted to us (Matthew 18:27, 33). The parable of indebtedness has a real significance to our present study in that it illustrates how one man had the position to forgive the other man's debt and was also moved by pity to do so. The tragic twist to the story is that this very man whose debt was forgiven then found himself in the position to be able to forgive another's debt. He, however, was not moved by pity to do so. The end result was that he was removed from his position because of a lack of pity.

Because of compassionate pity, Jesus reached out to the needs of the human soul through teaching them (Matthew 9:36, Mark 6:34) and ministering directly to their brokenness and sorrows (Mark 9:22, Luke 7:13). Jesus gave illustrations to motivate us to display compassion equal to the compassionate love of our Heavenly Father. (Luke 15:20) In the spiritual dimension, Jesus was moved to ministry when compassion compelled Him to cast out demons (Mark 5:19), forgive sins (Romans 9:15), and heal crippling wounds (Hebrews 5:2). His compassion was publicly demonstrated when He took time to talk with the outcast woman at the Samaritan well, when He stopped to defend and then justify the woman who was caught in the very act of committing adultery, and when a physical tear rolled down His cheek at Lazarus' memorial service. Then, He spelled out to His followers that it is exactly this same quality of pity that He will look for in them when He evaluates their lives. The sheep who are invited into the pleasures of heaven for eternity and the goats who are doomed to eternal judgment and suffering are separated based upon one simple criterion--their acts of compassion or pity.

During their walk with Jesus, the disciples were so accustomed to participating in charitable works that their first thought when Judas left the table at the Last Supper was that he was going to contribute to the poor. This practice of public charity apparently spilled over into their lives after the death, burial, resurrection, and ascension of the Lord. Peter and John's response to the beggar's appeal indicated that they would have willingly offered him silver and gold had they had any with them. Even as early as Acts chapter six, we see that the New Testament had instituted an organized ministry of compassion to care for widows.

This same motivation of compassion can be traced through the annals of church history which are filled with the "George Mueller"s who have taken in the destitute by the thousands, the "Mother Teresa"s who loved the poorest of the poor, and the "Bob Pierce's who have prayed, "Let my heart be broken by the things that break the heart of God."--men and women who made a difference.

But there are a couple special scriptures we must consider. One from the thirteenth chapter of First Corinthians warns us that good deeds for charity's purposes alone are useless. Paul said that there is no profit in giving all our resources to feed the poor if done from the wrong motivation, while at the same time the apostle James warns us that neither is there any benefit if we offer a person in need the spiritual benediction to go and be warmed and fed but do not put feet to our prayers. (verse 2:6) In other words, prayers without action are useless and actions without the proper motivation are also useless. Let's take a look at one short case study to see how all these elements must fit together in the life of a man who can make a difference.

In the year of 1931, a young evangelist was waiting to be given the pulpit in the little country school house in rural Tennessee where he was to preach. Suddenly he lost sight of everything around him and was transported into a visionary state. Not much is known of what happened in the physical realm that night because he was too embarrassed to ask anyone how they conducted the rest of the meeting when the preacher was in a trance. All he knew is that several hours later, he came to himself in the dark because someone in the congregation had taken the kerosene lantern with him when they left the building. But, in the spiritual realm some very important revelations were being instilled into the "little preacher" as the local farmers loved to call him. That night, Lester Sumrall saw the nations of the world marching down the highway to hell and being pushed off the abrupt end of the pavement into an abyss of liquid fire. He was also shown a vision of his own hands stained with the blood of those who were tumbling over that precipice into a Godless eternity.

During the agonizing hours in which the young preacher rolled on the dirt floor until his white suit was stained red from the clay, he had a heart transformation which proved to be one of his most valuable keys to his life and ministry: compassion. Until that fateful night, Lester would readily admit that he was preaching simply to stay alive because the Lord had directed that the only thing that stood between him and his grave was the gospel message he was commanded to preach. He had no regard for the eternal destiny of his congregation. In fact, he sometimes walked off and left penitents at the altar without ministering to or praying for them. But on that night, he became obsessed with the destiny of the souls of men.

He often said that the only thing that mattered was souls--not television stations (although he built an entire network of Christian television stations plus a world-wide network of short-wave stations and a twenty-four-hour-a-day satellite broadcasting system), not buildings (although the country is dotted with television stations he built and three impressive church edifices stand as memorials to his ministry in South Bend, Indiana, Hong Kong, and Manila), not books (although he authored over one hundred books and study guides), not money (although his organization became a multi-million-dollar operation)--only souls. It was his constant determination that he would do nothing nor own anything which did not produce souls for the Kingdom of God. To Lester Sumrall, people were not just numbers or statistics--they were the very individuals whom he saw plunging off the highway of life and being catapulted into a Christless eternity of torment; they were the blood which trickled through his fingers in that sobering vision. To Lester Sumrall, people were human beings who desperately needed and deserved his love and concern. Even as an internationally renown evangelist, he did not consider himself too important to stop and chat with the carpet cleaner in a hotel. That man was one of the men from the road in his vision; he was one of the men for whom Jesus and Lester Sumrall had pity and compassion.

Though he gained a genuine pity for the souls of men, Lester Sumrall still lacked a compassion for their physical needs. I will never forget sitting in the room with him as he slid a check across his desk to a missionary who runs feeding centers in one of the impoverished nations of Asia. Along with the check came the words, "God hasn't called me to feed the devil's children, and I don't believe in this sort of thing. When I go to the mission field, I don't see naked babies. But I'm giving you this for your work because I don't want the world to say that we don't try to help people." However, all that was to change late one evening in Jerusalem.

Soon after retiring after a long day of touring and taping television programs followed by preaching and ministering to the tour members, he was suddenly awakened by the words, "It is not only ten minutes to midnight in Jerusalem; it is ten minutes to midnight prophetically!" For the next five hours, the Lord continued to talk with His servant concerning a new commission of establishing a global ministry to feed the hungry saints who lack their daily bread. At first he retorted that he was seventy-five years old and that God should get a younger man to take on this job. Eventually he understood that God had saved this job for him until this stage in life because he was now seasoned enough to take on a project of this immensity. From that moment until the day he drew his last breath, Lester Sumrall poured every bit of energy he had into seeing that this vision would be fulfilled.

Upon his return to the US a few days later, I again sat in the apostle's office and witnessed him slide a piece of paper across his desk. This time, it was a page from a yellow legal pad totally filled with the words the Lord had spoken to him that night in Jerusalem. But the paper contained not just words, but huge smears where warm tears had dissolved the ink--evidence of a heart in which a new level of pity and compassion had been birthed. When this new element became operative in his ministry, Lester Sumrall stepped to a new level in his career as a man who made a difference. Because of this new birth of pity, he was able to impact thousands on every continent of the world in the last few years of his life and bring influential change to whole nations and people groups. The words of the apostle Jude so adequately sum up this case study, "Some have compassion, making a difference." (verse 22)

This quality of compassionate pity is such a necessary trait in the lives of those who wish to make a difference that the Apostle James mentions it as the summation of what our faith is all about. "Pure religion and undefiled before God and the Father is this, To visit the fatherless and widows in their affliction..." (verse 1:27) In the same breath he continues, "and to keep himself unspotted from the world." This segways directly in to the next nonnegotiable quality--purity.

People of Purity

"What is going on?" The question kept cycling through his head. "Why is this man talking like this? Doesn't he know that this is almost certainly the last time he'll ever be able to teach us? Doesn't he know that we have all traveled a long way and put out a lot of effort to be here today? Why is he using these few precious minutes to talk about what he has and hasn't done?"

Our friend had been one of the Apostle Paul's followers since the day the preacher showed up on the pleasant Mediterranean shores of Ephesus. Having been a disciple of Apollos who had introduced him to the teachings of John the Baptist, he had eagerly welcomed the evangelist known as a leading spokesman for the new movement that was revitalizing the Jewish faith--that is, when he wasn't stirring up a riot among the Jews who didn't want their faith revitalized. Our friend knew that John the Baptist had told his followers that he was only a messenger to announce the Promised One and that he was expecting to decrease so that the Promised One would be able to increase. Apollos had done an excellent job of showing from the Old Testament how all the prophets had pointed to the same message that John had taught. The only problem was that Apollos didn't know if John had ever revealed who this Promised One was. As far has he knew, King Herod had beheaded the camel-skin-clad preacher before he had been able to identify Him. The day when this new preacher showed up in town made our friend almost giddy with excitement as he wondered if he might be able to help answer some of the questions Apollos had left dangling.

Almost as soon as the new preacher opened his mouth, our friend and his eleven companions realized that he had much to teach them, but it was when he mentioned the Holy Spirit that they realized that not only were they not on the same page with their new teacher--they weren't even in the same textbook. He had patiently taken them through all the basics and brought them "up to speed" on the new faith. Although he had been baptized by Apollos in the method that John had taught, our friend enthusiastically splashed his way into the creek to be baptized in the name of Jesus in acceptance of Paul's teachings. Not only that, he had ecstatically begun to speak with unknown tongues as he came up out of the water--baptized not only in the creek, but also in the Holy Spirit which he had only heard of for the first time that day. From that moment on, our friend felt as if he had been joined to the apostle like a Siamese twin. He was with him almost every day over the next three months as he found himself in the local synagogues reasoning with the Jews and then over the next two years as the apostle taught each day in Tyrannus' school building.

What powerful times those were. Every lesson was a new revelation of incredible wisdom as the man who had learned at the feet of the great rabbi Gamaliel, and then taught by the Holy Spirit Himself in the desert of Arabia, exposed truth after truth from the Old Testament and showed how they had been fulfilled through the messiah, Jesus of Nazareth. Oh, what wisdom had flowed from his lips every time he opened his mouth. And what powerful miracles followed his words: people being supernaturally healed and set free from demonic control--even without his personally ministering to them, but by simply sending handkerchiefs to them!

His wisdom, authoritative teachings, and miraculous deeds had motivated everyone to such unimaginable heights that they soon were spreading the gospel like an epidemic throughout all Asia Minor until they considered that everyone in the region had heard the message within just two short years. In fact, the gospel had taken such root that some of the local artisans who made their living by selling trinkets at the temple of Diana actually feared that they would go into bankruptcy because so few people were visiting the shrine because they had begun to believe the apostle's message that there is no living god except Jesus. The resulting citywide riot focused on trying to silence this eloquent teacher eventually culminated in Paul's miraculous deliverance from a Daniel-versus-the-lions-style encounter.

When he eventually left the city, our friend had kept in touch with his mentor through his messengers such as Aquilla, Pricilla, Timothy, and Tychicus; but today, after hearing that the apostle wanted to meet the leaders of the Ephesian church in Miletus as he was traveling to Jerusalem, he had eagerly trekked the forty-six miles for one last visit with his teacher. But no matter how exciting it was to see his master's face again, he was perplexed at the message the apostle had chosen to share. There was nothing of the revelatory insight into the theological mysteries of the gospel, nothing of the stories of the glorious feats of healing or deliverance, no testimonies of the spread of the gospel among the gentiles and Jews alike. Instead, the revered teacher was sharing only about how he had lived among the followers in Ephesus.

> Ye know, from the first day that I came into Asia, after what manner I have been with you at all seasons, Serving the Lord with all humility of mind, and with many tears, and temptations, which befell me by the lying in wait of the Jews: And how I kept back nothing that was profitable unto you, but have shewed you, and have taught you publickly, and from house to house, testifying both to the Jews, and also to the Greeks, repentance toward God, and faith toward our Lord Jesus Christ…Wherefore I take you to record this day, that I am pure from the blood of all men. For I have not shunned to declare unto you all the counsel of God…Remember, that by the space of three years I ceased not to warn every one night and day with tears…I have coveted no man's silver, or gold, or apparel. Yea, ye yourselves know, that these hands have

ministered unto my necessities, and to them that were with me. (Acts 20:18-35)

As Paul was wrapping up his personal ministry to the church, he turned to the one significant factor which genuinely validated his work among them--his purity. He knew that without integrity of character, none of his brilliant teachings, supernatural experiences, or mind-boggling exploits would be of any real significance. So in this last visit with the church elders that he loved so much, he wanted to leave them with a validation of his ministry and a directive of how they could similarly confirm their work and lives--purity of motive and action.

Lack of purity will spoil everything else that might be positive in your life. We've mentioned David a couple times as we have examined various qualities of people who make a difference; however, we need to turn to the record of his life again to see how his failure in this one area overrode the other qualities which were in place. When the king's wandering eyes brought his neighbor's wife to David's bedroom and his scheming heart sent his neighbor to his grave, the prophet Nathan declared that the sword would never depart from David's house as a punishment for his sins. (II Samuel 12:10) As a result of this sin, David was never able to know peace from his conflicts and conquests, a factor that kept him from being able to fulfill one of the greatest of his dreams--to build a temple in Jerusalem to house the Ark of the Covenant. (I Kings 5:3; I Chronicles 22:8, 28:3) The impact of this story is that David had drawn up all the plans for the temple and collected billions of dollars worth of gold, silver, and building materials for this project, but he was forbidden from even initiating it. (I Chronicles 15:12, 22:14, 28:11-21, 29:2-3) He had the position, the plan, the provision, and passion; but he lacked purity--the key element that disqualified him from doing the project.

In recent history, we have witnessed the demise of a number of great men of God--men whose lives were flaming examples of passion, purpose, position, and power.

However, their compromises in terms of their purity undid all that they had accomplished with all their other God-given qualities. When the sins of one of these men were exposed, I was ministering in India--a Hindu nation on the opposite side of the world. Yet, even there, every sordid detail of the whole matter was splashed out unashamedly in all the headlines. When I returned to the States a few days later, I visited a bookstore which usually carried shelves full of his books, only to find that it seemed as if this once renowned author had never even existed. Nothing inside any of his books had changed. The truths and lessons were just as powerful and life-changing as they had been before his hidden life was brought to light, but suddenly they were no longer of value. The tragic truth is that once a man is discredited, so is his message and his ministry.

Paul knew this. That is why his last words to the church leaders whom he loved so deeply were to validate his purity of motives and action. That's why he included the element of unquestionable character as a qualifier for his ministry to the Thessalonian church. "For our gospel came not unto you in word only, but also in power, and in the Holy Ghost, and in much assurance; as ye know what manner of men we were among you for your sake." (I Thessalonians 1:5)

People who wish to make a difference must always remember that there is nothing that they do in private that will ever escape being revealed. (Numbers 32:23, Ecclesiastes 10:20, Luke 12:2) When their hidden lives are exposed, <u>it</u> will make a difference in whether <u>they</u> will make a difference!

People of Prayer

It was one of those evenings that you would expect when a bunch of "good old boys" get together--a dozen guys and a hundred belly laughs as they poked fun at one another and pulled practical jokes at each other's expense. One of the bunch taunted, "Did you hear what the teacher said today? He said that we would eventually be able to do even more outstanding things than he does. If that's the case--Peter, you need to work on your walking-on-water lessons. Those three steps you made before starting to gulp water don't qualify as being too outstanding! You should have paid attention to the hey-kids-don't-try-this-at-home disclaimer." Without missing a beat, Peter lashed back, "Well, it might have been a few steps, but at least I did actually walk on that water. I don't seem to remember any of the rest of you doing anything other than just sitting on your big fat bottoms in the boat!! But while we are at it, what about the day that James and John and I were with the teacher up on the mountain and the father of that little epileptic boy asked all the rest of you to try to cast out the devil. When we got back down the mountain, we didn't see any outstanding works. It looked more like a bunch of slapstick comics bumbling around than a convention of power-packed men of God!!" About that time, John chimed into the lighthearted fun but with a more sobering tone that turned the whole conversation to a serious note, "But remember what the teacher said when all this happened? He said that we would only be able to do things like set that little boy free through prayer. John the Baptist and other great teachers give their students lessons on prayer. But, even though we always see him up early praying and staying up pretty late to pray, we've never had a real class on the topic from the teacher. Maybe we should ask him to teach us; maybe this will actually be the key to being able to do all these great things that he tells us we will eventfully be able to do.[2]

It is true that people who make a difference are always people of prayer. Mark Twain immortalized the idea that everybody talks about the weather but nobody does anything about it. That must be because no one ever told him about Jeremiah who prayed earnestly that it might not rain and it didn't rain for three and a half years and then he prayed again and brought on a flood. (James 5:17-18) Anyone who wants to influence his world can take a clue from this great man of God and the cast of thousands of lesser known but just as significant prayer warriors of history and contemporary time. Prayer must be the hallmark of the lives of those who make a difference. Ephesians 6:18 admonishes us to pray all the time, I Timothy 2:8 directs us to pray everywhere, I Timothy 2:1 commands us to pray for everyone, Mark 11:24 instructs us to pray for everything, Ephesians 6:18 teaches us to pray with every kind of prayer, and a multitude of verses (Ephesians 6:18, Romans 8:26-18, I Corinthians 14:14-15) instruct us to pray in the Spirit.

When Dick Eastman, one of today's leading authorities on prayer, was challenged with the argument that the things he reported as answers to prayer were simply coincidences, he responded, "Well, more coincidences seem to happen the more I pray." It may seen truly simple, but it is simply true that prayer changes things. If we want to be men and women who see things change in the world around us, we must be men and women who see them change in our prayers.

---

[2] OK, the chronology of the gospels makes it impossible for this conversation to have ever occurred. But give me a break; it's just a story!

People with Power

Today started like any other day. A friend had to help drag him to his usual spot just outside the Beautiful Gate in the temple compound where he had spent every day for the past several decades; whether there was bone-chilling drizzle or the relentless skin-parching blazing sun, he had staked out the same little corner where an endless parade of devotees would pass as they came to worship in the temple. But today was to be different--not because the day was different or because the man was different, but because he was to meet a couple of men who had what it takes to make a difference in their worlds. When he first noticed the men, there was nothing about them that indicated that they were anything special or that anything special was about to happen. So, our friend went through his well rehearsed ritual of making a pathetic grimace and sticking out his battered little cup to receive a few loose coins. But then it happened--the one thing that changed his whole life. The would-be benefactor held out his hand, but his palm was up, not down as it would be were he ready to drop a coin into the waiting cup. The upturned palm was accompanied by the astonishing words, "I don't have any money, but I do have something even better. In the name of Jesus, get up and start walking!" With that reverberating command, he grabbed our friend's hand, jerking him to his feet. The whole thing happened so quickly that he almost didn't have time to realize what had happened. He certainly didn't have time to protest that he couldn't get up because he was crippled. The next thing he knew, he was not only standing; he was walking--and not only walking; he was actually jumping up and down like some kind of acrobat. Next he was running. Before he realized what was going on, he found himself rushing into the temple itself--a sanctuary which had been denied him for so many years because of his disability. So elated over the miraculous healing he had just experienced, he forgot himself and ran through the sacred compound shouting and making a spectacle of himself, astonishing everyone present with the supernatural event that should have been associated with such a holy place but hadn't been seen here for centuries.

But, wait a minute! These two men weren't exactly strangers. Our friend was certain that he had seen them before. In fact, he was sure that they were frequent temple visitors who came regularly for prayers and that they had often paused just long enough to drop a coin into his little alms cup. So what had happened in these men that make them so different this day as from all the calendar of previous days? This day they were different--they were men with power. It turned out that these men were from the group that had caused an incredible stir just a few days before during the festival of Pentecost. Boy, talk about days being different from other days; what a day that one was! These guys and another hundred or so of their friends were all over the temple compound causing at least as big a stir as our friend had just done as he raced around the premises showing off his healing. They were screaming and yelling in all kinds of different languages, amazing the folks who had traveled from just about everywhere to attend the holiday celebrations. It seems that everyone realized that these folks had never studied these foreign languages, yet they were speaking them fluently by some inexplicable force. Then one of them stepped forward and took over the show to preach about Jesus. Oh, that was him! Yes, the guy who had just done this miracle--he was the one who had captivated the multitudes and influenced a sea of them to convert to his Jesus. But why was he so intoxicatingly influential that day and so authoritatively effective today when he had seemed like any other guy before? What had made him a man of power? What had made him a man with supernatural ability to make a difference?

This man Peter had received the power that Jesus had promised to him through being filled with the Holy Spirit. (Acts 1:8; 10:38; 2:22, 43; 4:30; 5:12; 14:3; Romans 15:19; II

Corinthians 12:12; Hebrews 2:4) It was the power that made a difference in his life--changing him from the cowardly man who whimpered when a little girl challenged him (Luke 22:55) to a stalwart hero who could brazenly defy the national rulers (Acts 5:29). Not only did this encounter with the Holy Spirit make a difference in Peter's life, it also transformed him into a man who was to make a difference in the lives of all he met, even to the point of healing people who were just touched by his shadow! (Acts 5:15)

The whole of Christian history is marked by people who have made a difference because they were people of power. A very prominent story comes from the life of Dr. Lester Sumrall. When the Lord spoke to him to go to the Philippines to raise up a ministry there, He promised, "I will do more for you there than I have done for you anywhere else in your ministry." Knowing that there had never been any major Protestant revival in the Philippines in the history of the country and that there were very few Christians in the city, Bro. Sumrall went to Manila with great anticipation of what God was going to do. For the first several months, there was only a handful of people in his church. About the time that he had built the congregation up to around fifty people, the Lord began impressing upon him that he was to build a barn to hold the coming harvest. So he started building a church that would seat twenty-five hundred people. He reasoned that he needed a building of at least that size since he had left a church in the US with over a thousand adults and a thousand children in the Sunday school each week and the Lord had promised something bigger in the Philippines. Everybody begged him not to do it. His denomination thought he would make them the laughing stock of the entire world--building a church to seat over two thousand when he only had fifty members. Protestant missionaries and prominent church leaders came to Manila to stop him because they were afraid he would take their members to fill his church. But he refused to be swayed by their arguments because he knew that God would bring a revival such as the Philippines had never seen.

One night as he was getting ready for bed, he listened to the evening news. Suddenly, blood-curdling screaming and horrifying howls come across the airwaves. The news feature was the story of a young girl incarcerated in the Bilibid Prison in Manila who had been mysteriously bitten by unseen teeth. Medical doctors and prison wardens observed as tooth marks and blood mysteriously appeared on her body. From his other missionary work, Bro. Sumrall recognized that this was demon power tormenting her, so he got out of bed and laid in the floor praying and travailing, asking God to send somebody to deliver her from the demon power. But the Lord answered him, "If you don't do it, it won't happen. You are the only one in this city who knows how to cast the devil out of her." After spending that night in prayer and fasting, he called the contractor who was building the church. Because this gentleman was a personal friend of the mayor, he arranged for Bro. Sumrall to have an audience with the mayor where he asked permission to go into the Bilibid prison to pray for the girl. The story of the girl had already hit the international news, and the city had sent out appeals for church leaders, psychiatrists, or somebody to come and help her--but no one was able to deliver her. Bro. Sumrall went to pray for her, but he did not get a total victory the first day; so he went back again the second and third days. After three days of fasting and prayer he spoke to the spirit, and it left. But not only was the girl set free, a remarkable thing happened in the city. Unbeknownst to Bro. Sumrall, the demon spirit that was controlling that young girl was the principality spirit that ruled the entire Philippines. And as soon as his power was broken, the entire spirit realm of the Philippines became defenseless against the attack of the gospel. When Bro. Sumrall was ushered back into the mayor's office with the good news that the girl had been freed, the mayor was so pleased that he asked what Bro. Sumrall wanted in return. His request was for permission to have large open air revival meetings every night on the main plaza of the city. Within a six-week period, one hundred fifty thousand people were converted to Christ. When construction of the church was complete and the dedication service was held, the church was so jam packed that all the people could not get inside.

Another phenomenal story of a man who made a difference because of the power of the Holy Spirit in his life comes from the year 1956 when Tommy Hicks, a little-know evangelist, was invited to Argentina. On the flight down, he was directed by the Holy Spirit to pray for a gentleman named "Peron." It turned out that the "Peron" he was to find and minister to was the president of the country. When the evangelist showed up at the presidential palace to ask for permission to see the president, he was questioned as to what business he had trying to meet with President Peron. When Hicks explained that he was there as a messenger from God with a gift of healing, the guard asked for prayer. Upon being instantly healed, the guard made arrangements for the evangelist to meet with the president, who was also miraculously healed as onlookers watched the healing manifest. Argentina was rocked under the seismic impact of the healing crusade. Any time a critic would speak against the revival, ten people would stand up and testify to what they had personally experienced.

Even in such remote settings as a village in Tamil Nadu State in southern India, the power of the Holy Spirit makes a difference and causes men to make a difference in others' lives. A little white-haired Indian man had been trying year after year to evangelize his Hindu village for Christ. Yet, the people's hearts and ears were closed. Finally, one day at an evangelism training conference in the city of Madras (now know as Chennai), he learned the principle of the Great Commission--that we are to go forth in the power of the Holy Spirit as well as with the truth of the Word of God. Returning to his village with a new power from his new relationship with the Holy Spirit, he found that an old lady in the village had been gored by a water buffalo.

Laying his hands on her, he commanded that she be totally healed. Instantly, her crippled legs received strength and her mangled body was straightened. Since the whole village had seen the woman's condition after the attack and then saw her miraculous recovery, everyone suddenly believed that the old man's message was real. The village that had rejected his testimony for years was converted overnight! Because the Holy Spirit made a difference in him, he was able to make a difference in his village.

People of Perseverance

The two men caught each other's eyes as they both swallowed hard. They could barely believe their ears. Were they really hearing the verdict that they were being sentenced to forty years without a possibility for early parole? They were especially astonished because the sentence was being declared by a judge who knew personally that they were innocent of any wrongdoing. Subject to guilt by association, Caleb and Joshua were doomed to spend the next forty years of their lives wandering through the Sinai Desert with the true perpetrators--the ten other spies who gave negative reports after their recognizance mission into the Promised Land and the masses who had accepted their pessimistic evaluation. Though Caleb and Joshua had made every effort possible to encourage the people to aggressively go after the Promised Land, they were now destined to suffer the same consequences as the true culprits who had to legitimately pay for their rebellion against God's directive. However, these two men had one all-important quality that made them able to bear the unjust sentence--perseverance. This quality of persistence made these two men able to hang onto the promises of God until they saw them become realities. This quality guaranteed their permanence in spite of all they had to endure. In fact, this quality not only gave them enduring power, it gave them the triumphing muscle to be the ones who, despite the fact that they were octogenarians by this time, were the leaders to actually take the masses into the Promised Land. Joshua led the full invasion while Caleb, essentially single-handedly, took a mountain that he had set his eye on some four decades earlier.

> Then the children of Judah came unto Joshua in Gilgal: and Caleb the son of Jephunneh the Kenezite said unto him, Thou knowest the thing that the LORD said unto Moses the man of God concerning me and thee in Kadeshbarnea. Forty years old

was I when Moses the servant of the LORD sent me from Kadeshbarnea to espy out the land; and I brought him word again as it was in mine heart. Nevertheless my brethren that went up with me made the heart of the people melt: but I wholly followed the LORD my God. And Moses sware on that day, saying, Surely the land whereon thy feet have trodden shall be thine inheritance, and thy children's for ever, because thou hast wholly followed the LORD my God. And now, behold, the LORD hath kept me alive, as he said, these forty and five years, even since the LORD spake this word unto Moses, while the children of Israel wandered in the wilderness: and now, lo, I am this day fourscore and five years old. As yet I am as strong this day as I was in the day that Moses sent me: as my strength was then, even so is my strength now, for war, both to go out, and to come in. Now therefore give me this mountain, whereof the LORD spake in that day; for thou heardest in that day how the Anakims were there, and that the cities were great and fenced: if so be the LORD will be with me, then I shall be able to drive them out, as the LORD said. And Joshua blessed him, and gave unto Caleb the son of Jephunneh Hebron for an inheritance. Hebron therefore became the inheritance of Caleb the son of Jephunneh the Kenezite unto this day, because that he wholly followed the LORD God of Israel. (Joshua 14:6-14)

People who make a difference must be like Joshua and Caleb who, even though they had to put up with forty years in the desert because of other people's unbelief, kept their faith and eventually entered and possessed the Promised Land. The prize is given only to the one who finishes the course. The promise of salvation is relegated to those who endure to the end. (Matthew 10:22)

Winston Churchill once addressed a class of graduating college seniors at their commencement by gruffly charging them, "Never give up!" He took a deep breath and bellowed out a second time, "Never give up!" Then after his third demand that they never give up, he took his seat. Winston Churchill led England to victory in World War II because he refused to give up; he made a difference. More dramatically, he inspired his generation to grasp the principle of perseverance so that the whole nation was inspired to make a difference in their present world.

People Who Believe in Their Personal Witness

He couldn't remember all the details. After all, he was just a little child when most of it happened--and adults just don't let kids in on much of the kind of stuff that was going on. But he could never forget the terror of it all. He supposed it had something to do with wine, but there must have been more than that because this sort of thing didn't happen to others who enjoyed the bottle. He could remember how that almost every family get-together ended in chaos with Uncle Legion ranting and raving angrily about something. Usually, he didn't understand what all was going on because his mother would hurry to huddle him and the other small children into another room. Often, he would hear the crashing of furniture being broken and the sounds of a scuffle as the uncle had to be dragged out of the house. He remembered one time when he and his cousins tried to peek through the crack in the door to see what was going on. Had it not been for the fact that they were panting so hard in horror, they would have wanted to giggle at the sight of this one uncle ripping off all his clothes and their other uncles having to struggle the naked man to the floor. Our friend would strain to listen when his mom and her brothers and sisters would speak in hushed tones about the uncle, but then he would wish that he hadn't strained so hard when cold chills would rush up his spine every time he heard them whisper the word "demon." As bad as all this was, things turned worse after his grandmother died. Uncle Legion would wonder around the house muttering something about Grandma sending him messages from beyond the grave. Then he would disappear for days--sometimes even weeks--at the time. The rumor was that he was living in the cemetery so he could hear from his departed mother. Although our friend was never sure why anyone ever wanted to bring him back to town, he could remember times when his dad and uncles recruited several other strong men from the village to go out to the graveyard to catch him and tie him up and bring him home. The story that was told about these little adventures is that Uncle Legion tossed the men around with superhuman strength and somehow managed to break loose no matter how strong of ropes they had used.

But--and this is the must astonishing "but" you can imagine--all that had changed in one single day when a man named Jesus visited the region where Uncle Legion was holed up and somehow sent all the evil that was raging in the madman's mind and body into a herd of swine! Except for the fact that this was his own uncle and he had seen him in his insane rages so many times, our friend would have had a hard time imaging that this story could possibly be true. As for the pigs--well, he knew all the people who actually saw them drown after they rushed over the cliff like lemmings committing mass suicide.[3]

Uncle Legion had asked Jesus to let him travel with him as he ministered around the Galilee and as far away as Jerusalem; but when the teacher had refused him permission, Legion's eyes, which had a sparkle of life for the first time in years, grew a bit darker as his hopes were shattered and crashed to the ground. Instead, the teacher wanted Legion to return to his home and family. When he understood that he had a mission among his own family and friends, the sparkle came blazing back and his hope was totally restored. Legion gave up that nickname immediately and rushed back to his village to show everyone what had happened in his life. It was probably the happiest day in Mamma's life when her brother came walking through the door with his hair trimmed and combed, dressed neatly, and wearing a beaming smile. Boy, it certainly made a difference for our friend and his cousins; the uncle that once terrorized them became their favorite. He always seemed to have a new game to play or something else fun "up his sleeve" and some hilarious story to tell. Plus, he was always rushing off to some place to tell people about what

---

[3] Of course I know that lemmings don't really commit suicide, but you do have to admit that the idea does add a bit of flavor to the story.

had happened to him and how Jesus had set him free from it; then, he would come back home with some eye-popping story about what had happened on his journey. Before long, his story was known throughout all ten of the Greek-speaking cities in the region. In fact, it was because of his story that such a large crowd came to see Jesus the next time his travels brought him back this way. Wow, what an event that turned out to be--over four thousand of them were supernaturally fed with just seven pieces of bread and a few fish. But that's another story for another time.

      Legion demonstrates another powerful principle in the lives of those who make a difference--the power of personal witness. As far as we know, Legion never preached a public sermon; however, it was the testimony of what had happened in his life that brought thousands together to hear Jesus the next time He was in the region. Billy Graham once said that--in spite of the fact that he spent hundreds of thousands of dollars on television and radio time, newspaper ads, billboards, and church bulletin inserts to promote his great evangelistic campaign--eight-five percent of the people who attended came out as the result of a personal invitation. If we want to be people who make a difference, we must always keep our focus on personal contact with individuals. In trying to change a nation, we can't forget that every nation is made up of individuals. If we make a difference in the lives of individuals, we eventfully make a difference in the community and the nation. Like when a stone is tossed into a pond and the ripples eventually touch the distant shore, our personal contact with individuals will eventually impact the whole of society.

People with Paper

His hands trembled as he reached out to take the document. Even though he was accustomed to handling top secret dossiers, top level files determining international policies, surrender treaties, terms-of-peace agreements, business contracts that represented seven and eight and sometimes even higher figures in the monetary exchange, decrees that placed some men in the highest posts in the nation, judgments that removed other men from their powerful positions, warrants that called suspects in for trial, and verdicts that cost some men their very lives; there was something different about the parchment that was being presented to him today. In comparison to this dusty old manuscript, any other document he had ever handled seemed to be nothing more than just a piece of paper with words scrawled on it. This scroll, however, was not the decree of a king, the bench ruling of a judge, the plans of an architect, or the edict of a lawmaker--it was the decree of the King of Kings, the verdict of the One who sits at the bench of the White Throne Judgment, the master plan of the Architect of the Universe, the mandate of the Great Lawgiver--it was the very Word of God!

The twenty-six-year-old King Josiah nervously took the parchment from the hands of his scribe Shaphan who had served as courier to bring it from the high priest Hilkiah. The forgotten document had been discovered hidden somewhere inside the temple which was being renovated under Josiah's directive as part of his attempt to reform the nation. After a lingering moment of awe as he held the sacred scroll, the king instructed the scribe to read the document to him. Servants hurriedly arranged a chair for Shaphan and a lounge for the king. In as composed a voice as he could muster, the scribe began to read. The air was heavy with tension and anxiety as the words fell on the monarch's ears. Each syllable seemed to bear an indictment against the rebellion and idolatry of the people over whom Josiah reigned. And with each new revelation of the judgment looming over the heads of his nation, the king's anguish intensified. Finally, the geyser of turmoil within him erupted as he leapt to his feet and rent his clothes as an outward sign of his internal anxiety. In response to having understood the consequences spelled out in the book of the law, the king led the people in making a covenant before the Lord to keep His commandments with all their hearts and souls and to perform all the words of the covenant that were written in the book.   The Bible sums up Josiah's life by saying, "And like unto him was there no king before him, that turned to the LORD with all his heart, and with all his soul, and with all his might, according to all the law of Moses; neither after him arose there any like him" (II Kings 23:25)--all the result of one piece of paper!

People who make a difference are people who recognize and utilize the power of the printed page. Over half of the Christians in the world attribute their salvation to the printed page, a testimony to the power of the scripture and proof that the Word of God doesn't lose its power with time. One furniture mover came to Christ by reading a tract he found under a sofa he was moving out of a house. That little voiceless witness had been hidden there for about twenty-two years. One gospel publishing company reported receiving mail at an old address which they hadn't used for twenty-four years, indicating that their tracts were still in circulation and doing their job a quarter of a century later.

Dr. Sumrall told the story about a Protestant missionary who was giving away Bibles in a predominately Catholic region. The local priest was so enraged that a Protestant had invaded his "territory" that he snatched one of the Bibles from the missionary's hand, ripped it to shreds, and threw the pieces into the gutter. A local vegetable vendor reclaimed the pages to use as wrapping paper for the produce he sold at his stand. As the local women unwrapped their vegetables, they began to read the pages and visit their neighbors to try to find the rest of the story. Before long, the entire village was engaged in a giant game of jigsaw puzzle as they tried to reassemble the testament. As the people read the story of the book, the whole village became aflame with a revival that eventually brought the entire village to Christ.

Similarly amazing stories come from all corners of the earth. A man in a Latin American country was so angered by having been given a gospel tract that he ripped the pamphlet to pieces; however, that night he couldn't sleep as his mind kept replaying the incident. Eventually, he got out of bed and pieced the tract together again, read its message, and prayed the prayer to receive salvation. Another incredible story took place in a small village in north central India near the border of Nepal. It begins with a man who bought three cigarettes from a shopkeeper in this village. The shopkeeper took a scrap of paper from a large pile and wrapped the gentleman's purchase. When the man returned home and unwrapped his cigarettes, the wrapper caught his attention and he began to read. Suddenly he knew that he had never read anything like this in his life. But he also realized that part of the message was missing because he had only half the page. So, in the heat of the day, the man ran back to the shop and explained to the shopkeeper that he wanted the other half of the paper. The shopkeeper simply laughed, "You see those stacks over there? It might be in there and it might not. If you really want it, go ahead and look." For the next few hours, the cigarette smoker painstakingly took each piece from the pile and examined it. When he couldn't find the piece that matched his, he went through the entire stack again. Frustrated and dejected, he finally started slowly home. However, he suddenly remembered that on the paper there was an address in a town about twelve miles away, so he borrowed a bicycle and began the hot journey. It was very late that day when he finally found the address and anxiously knocked. When a man answered, the cigarette smoker shouted at him, "Is this your address? Did you write this?" It took the man a few minutes to calm the cigarette smoker and explain that this was the right address but that he had not written the words; the words that had so impacted the man were from the Bible!

Another story of equal interest also involves a cigarette smoker. A missionary tried to sell a New Testament to a man in Zimbabwe who was obviously interested in the book; however, it turned out that he was not interested in the content of the New Testament but was eyeing the size of the pages and the texture of the paper. It was just the right size to use to roll his cigarettes. In fact, he told the missionary that he wouldn't buy it but would take it and use the pages for cigarette paper if he gave him the book. "I will make a deal with you," the missionary replied. "I will give you this book if you promise to read every page before you smoke it." Pleased with himself that he indeed had the better end of the bargain, the man took the New Testament and walked away. The missionary returned to his home country but years later attended a convention in Zimbabwe where the speaker on the platform recognized him in the audience. Pointing to him excitedly, he said, "This man doesn't remember me, but I remember him." He explained, "About fifteen years ago he tried to sell me a New Testament. When I refused to buy it, he gave it to me, even though I told him I would use the pages to roll cigarettes." He continued this strange testimony, saying, "I smoked Matthew. I smoked Mark. Then I smoked Luke. But when I got to John chapter three, verse sixteen, I couldn't smoke any more. My life was changed from that moment!" Now the former smoker is a full-time church evangelist devoting his life to showing others the way of salvation he found in this little book that had just the right size pages to roll cigarettes!

Glen Chambers was headed for Ecuador where he was going to serve as a first-term pioneer in the heart of the beautiful Andes Mountains. When his plane crashed leaving no survivors, all his friends and family lamented the tragic loss before he could even begin his mission work.

However, an unexpected twist came several years later when a stranger knocked on the door of Glen's mother's home. The young lady introduced herself as a missionary serving in Colombia where she was ministering among unreached people in remote villages. She explained that she was amazed when she came upon a village where there were already believers yet the people insisted that she was the first person ever to come to them with the gospel. They went on to say that several years prior to this, one of their men was hunting in the jungle when he found a badly burned little case, but inside of it was a book. The villagers read the book and believed its message. When the missionary looked at the slightly charred Spanish Bible, she found a dedication addressed to Glen Chambers and took note of the address. When she returned to the US, she determined to make it a point to share the story firsthand with Glen's mother proving the power of the written word even when a preacher isn't able to personally communicate it.

    A friend of mine from Nepal once wrote me about staying overnight in the same hotel where a Buddhist rimpoche (the highest ranking lama, or holy man) was also a guest. My friend said that he saw the lama seated, surrounded by his followers. With all the respect and reverence being accorded to him, he was apparently enjoying the recognition. My friend remembered a particularly large Bible he was carrying for just such an occasion, and--whispering a word of prayer--approached the holy man. After the preliminary introduction he respectfully asked him if he would like to have the most precious "postuk" (Nepali for "book"). When the rimpoche said that he would be delighted, my friend--in typical Nepali fashion--reached forward and presented him the Bible with both hands. Immediately the lama started to read and was engrossed with it--so much so that there was absolute silence. He continued reading on and on until his followers finally approached my friend, asking, "Sir, what kind of book did you give him? Look--it has been hours, and it is almost midnight. We are starving but cannot eat unless he eats first! Is it a magic book you gave him?"

In the Dominican Republic, some Bible college students were distributing gospel tracts on the street when a man came running out of a dentist office asking if he could have one. He had been in the dental chair having his teeth checked when he saw them through an open window. Still with the dental napkin penned around his neck, he rushed out to catch them before they disappeared around the corner.

Can you take just two more stories about the power of the printed word demonstrated in the remote regions of Nepal? One is set in a isolated village in the Himalayas where only one person--the Hindu priest is able to read. Since there is no electricity or any connection to the outside world, the one entertainment the people enjoy is to gather around the priest as he reads to them each evening after a hard day in the fields. Someone in the village somehow obtained a Bible which he asked the priest to read to them. Eventually, the entire village became Christians simply by hearing the scriptures read to them by, of all people, their Hindu priest! The other story comes from the tarai, the flatlands in the plains below the mountains. A pioneer missionary with Every Home for Christ trekked to this distant village which is a day and a half's walk from the nearest civilization center. Here, he gave a gospel tract to each family and left literature at the huts if no one was at home. Weeks later, a letter arrived at the EHC offices explaining that someone had found the pamphlet at his door when he returned that evening. He was so intrigued by its message that he walked the long journey into town to send a letter to the address on the back of the brochure. After several follow-up correspondences, an EHC worker decided to visit the village only to find that there was by then a group of four hundred believers -- none of whom had been witnessed to by any outside witness! It was all the result of that one little tract!

Long ago God gave a promise to His people, "For as the rain cometh down, and the snow from heaven, and returneth not thither, but watereth the earth, and maketh it bring forth and bud, that it may give seed to the sower, and bread to the eater: So shall my word be that goeth forth out of my mouth: it shall not return unto me void, but it shall accomplish that which I please, and it shall prosper in the thing whereto I sent it." (Isaiah 55:10-11) Unfortunately, much of the Christian world has failed to understand the power of the incorruptible seed of the Word of God (I Peter 1:23) on the printed page. The embarrassing indictment against us is that, when the Cold War was at its height, some researchers questioned why so many developing nations were embracing Communism and were told, "The Christians taught us to read, but the Communists gave us something to read." People who make a difference--whether it be positive or negative--are people who understand the power of the printed page.

People Who are Prejudice-free

"Let them laugh and make fun all they want to, but I know what it will take to win this war. It will take the blessing of God. And if having a woman with me on the front line is what I need to ensure that God's special favor is with me, then I'll have a woman right up front with me!!" With that brazen disregard for the opinion of all those who scorned him and made jokes about lace underwear and apron strings, Barak motioned for Deborah to take her place as the head of command of the troops as they headed for the battle. As they marched toward the enemy's encampment, Barak knew full well that a woman was going to get credit for the conquest, and when Jael drove a tent stake through Sisera's temple, all the accolades were heaped at her feet and the metals pinned on her chest. However, when the author of Hebrews recorded the role call of great Old Testament men and women of faith, he failed to remember either Deborah or Jael and listed only Barak when memorializing this victory. Why? Simply because Barak possessed and acted out of the next great quality of a person who makes a difference; he was prejudice-free.

Certainly, he would have looked a lot braver if he had courageously plowed toward the Canaanites without Deborah. And it is very likely that he would have won the battle; however, it is just as likely that his name would have been lost from the pages of history and his memory would have gone into oblivion. Instead, he demonstrated courage on two fronts--the physical battlefield against the enemy and the emotional battlefield against the opinions of men, even his own friends. Because he had the audacity to act against popular opinion, God preserved his name and honored his memory. By first winning the battle against prejudice and popular opinion, he was able to be victorious in the other conflicts facing him. Men and women who make a difference must overcome the prejudices that cripple the rest of society--whether they be prejudices against individuals because of their social standing, whole races because of their color, or half the human population because of their gender.

In his full African attire including cap, he looked rather austere as he sat across the table from us. The fact that he always introduced himself as "Bishop" made him seem even more pompous. But then when he challenged my wife during a dinner in our own home, I really thought that he was just too self-righteous. Biting her tongue, Peggy tried to calmly answer each of his objections and concerns. His problem was that he simply didn't agree that a woman had any place in the pulpit, and he emphasized that it would never happen in his country--and especially in his churches. About a year later, we sat across the same table as he shared another meal with my wife and me. But this time there was a marked difference. Much of the stuffiness was gone, and he spoke a bit less dogmatically as he addressed Peggy. "Sister," he said, "I must tell you what has happened in my churches. When I went back to Africa, I was concerned because of the lack of revival among my congregations. After much prayer, the Lord spoke to me and promised to tell me why there was no life among my people. He said, 'I created women to give birth, but you are keeping them barren!' Suddenly I realized that women were not only created to give physical birth; they were created to give spiritual birth as well. As long as I was barring them from ministry, I was keeping them barren. The lack of revival in my churches was my own fault because I had refused to allow the women to use their spiritual gifts and anointing. Since I have started allowing the women to serve as teachers, ministers, and cell leaders, my churches are all thriving and growing -- actually exploding!"

All of us know the end of Dr. David Yonggi Cho's story: a church of almost a million members; but few of us know the beginning of the story of when he reached a breaking point in his ministry because he was physically exhausted and spiritually drained. It was at this point that the Lord spoke to him that he needed helpers to share the load. What followed next was hard for him to accept and act upon: the Lord told him that the secret to his success and expansion would be through women. In his male-dominated oriental culture, he resisted that idea at first. Finally, he began to ask women to lead home cell groups and even to serve as associate pastors in his congregation. Now, the majority of his cell leaders--numbering in the thousands--and a large portion of his pastors--numbering in the hundreds--are women! It was through breaking the male-imposed bondage of barrenness off the women in his congregation that his church became an international wonder.

On my first mission trip to Nepal, I asked the top leaders of the emerging church what they saw as the greatest need in the national church. Their unhesitating response was that they needed someone to teach their women because their society had always kept women illiterate, forced them into servitude, and held them back in every way. From the very next mission, Peggy began to join me on my trips into the Himalayan kingdom, bringing other anointed ladies into the nation. These ladies on our team serve as examples of what women can accomplish for the Kingdom of God and bring deliverance, healing, encouragement, and challenge to the women in the church. Today, the Nepalese women have become one of the great forces moving the revival in the Kingdom of Nepal.

When Peggy and I were ministering at a conference for pastors and leaders who had gathered from six African nations, my wife's message drew as enthusiastic a response as could ever be expected--though maybe not as gracious as we might have hoped for. After noting that only a handful of the delegates were ladies, she had encouraged and challenged them to begin inviting women into active roles in their ministries and even into church leadership. She deliberately ended the session early to allow for questions--and did we ever have questions: If God wanted women in church leadership, why didn't He call a woman into the original twelve apostles? If you place a woman as the pastor of a church, what will she do when it is time to baptize new believers and there are big men who need to be baptized? Who said that women don't have to wear head coverings? This year you are telling us to ordain women; will you be telling us next year to ordain homosexuals? Talk about opening the proverbial can of worms--this time it was the whole barrel! As each question was dealt with honestly and with scriptural reference, the delegates began to see that we were not there to preach an American ideology but a biblical truth. The fact that Jesus and the apostles wanted to abstain from the very appearance of evil as they traveled and lived together in close quarters would not allow them to call a woman into their company. Just because the pastor is a woman doesn't mean that she has to be the one to personally baptize the converts. In I Corinthians 11:16, the Apostle Paul himself said that, although it was a custom for women to wear head coverings, it wasn't a requirement. Whereas the Bible specifically condemns homosexuality, it was God Himself who said that it was not good for men to be without women--a principle which extends beyond the home into the ministry. After reviewing the robust discussion engendered by the session, the director of the convention guaranteed me, "You'll see a difference when you come back next year. The sessions will be full of women ministers and pastors. These men heard what you said, and they want their churches to grow, so they will put your advice into practice."

     The history of the church is full of women who have made significant contributions to the cause of Christ. During the nineteenth century, prejudice at home kept women out of the pulpits of America and Europe, but opened the door for them in foreign fields, where the it apparently didn't matter since the audiences would have black or brown skin. These women did what many men could not have done--opening whole nations and tribal groups to the gospel. They were women like Lillian Trasher who cared for twelve hundred orphan children in Egypt, Mother Teresa whose Missionaries of Charity grew to over four thousand nuns operating more than six hundred missions in in over one hundred nations, Mary Slesser who almost single-handedly broke through the barriers of paganism, superstition, and tyranny in Nigeria, and Amy Carmichael who saved over a thousand young girls from forced prostitution in India. The chronicles of missions history are filled with the stories of great lady missionaries who literally conquered continents for the Kingdom of God. The truth is that many of the hinterland areas where men were reluctant to go were evangelized by little old ladies and young girls who willingly went despite the discomfort and danger. It may honestly be said that some of the best men on the mission field have been women!

    On the home front, a few brave and anointed women withstood the ridicule of the religious and the field day of the press who wished to make them look more like circus acts than gospel preachers. Maria Woodworth-Etter, Aimee Semple McPherson, and Kathryn Khulman stand out as giants today, but they suffered severe persecution as they broke out of the gender restrictions and became petticoats in the pulpits of early twentieth century America. These women accomplished remarkable victories for the Kingdom of God in spite of the fact that everything they achieved was in the face of misunderstanding, mistrust, slander, and opposition of every sort from the public media, the leaders of established religion, and even their own families.

    Though I've focused on prejudice against women, the truth is that any prejudice--whether it be rooted in gender, skin color, socio-economic differences, or any other factor--will hinder those who wish to make a difference. Live prejudice-free and become a man or woman who changes your world!

People of Prophecy

"Silly old fool!! I can't believe that the man is stupid enough to say such a thing! And what's worse, it looks like the king actually believes him! My word, don't they all know how desperate everything is? The whole world is collapsing around us, and this "prophet" is predicting that all our problems will be solved by this time tomorrow. Maybe the hunger has driven the man into some sort of delirium, and the king has been caught up into the deception with him. After all, people have actually turned to cannibalism to stay alive--and by cannibalism, I mean the worst thing imaginable: women eating their own babies!!! And this old fool is saying that in less than twenty-four hours we'll have so much food that it will sell for just pennies!! Why, even if bread started falling out of heaven like manna, these stupid prophecies couldn't be true. Well, anybody stupid enough to believe in this mumbo jumbo can just go ahead and starve to death for all I care!! It will serve him right!"

As the chief of staff and top intelligence officer, our friend should certainly know what he was talking about. But in reality, it didn't take a rocket scientist or a brain surgeon to come up with the same evaluation. Ever since the Syrian army had blockaded the city, Samaria had been in serious trouble. Since the barricade had stopped all deliveries of supplies and kept the people holed up inside the city walls, away from their fields and springs of water, the famine had gradually progressed as their stockpiles had dwindled. Every morsel of food and ounce of water had been carefully rationed until there was nothing left to ration. When all else was gone, the people turned to scraps of rubbish, shoe leather, and finally human flesh to sustain themselves. Yet, one man seemed certain that the end was in sight--and not just an end of the starvation; rather, he saw an abundant supply. But our friend was the king's special advisor, and it was his duty to protect the king from listening to such a madman; so he objected to the insane prediction. Elisha simply looked back and responded that every word he had spoken would certainly come to pass and that our friend would see it all happen but not get to taste one bite of the miraculous provision.

All the time, God was busily at work setting the stage for a supernatural supply for the Samaritans. He sent a panic among the enemy army, causing them to flee in terror and leave everything in their camp behind. Simultaneously four lepers stumbled upon the abandoned camp and discovered a treasure trove of food, supplies, and war spoils that the Syrians had taken in their earlier conquests. When these ostracized victims of society ventured back to the city and announced their serendipitous find, the king turned to his trusted advisor and appointed him to be in charge of collecting a gate fee from the people as they were to be allowed to enter the smorgasbord which had been the Syrian encampment. Apparently, the king failed to consult the rocket scientist and brain surgeon about this decision; otherwise, he would have immediately recognized the lunacy of expecting the people who were at the cannibalism stage of starvation, to stand orderly in line to pay their dues and wait for each customer's correct change to be made before they calmly strolled to the buffet table and politely took turns in the serving line. No, the scene was a stampede as everyone pushed and shoved to get to the head of the line. Driven by insatiable hunger, they clawed their way to the precious bounty, not allowing any obstacle--even the king's top advisor--to stand in their way. First an elbow in his side spun him out of his position at the gate; next came a knee to his groin that doubled him over in excruciating pain; then a full body tackle took him down to the dust. Before long all he could see was the soles of a million sandals trampling over him; eventually everything went black!

Well, our friend didn't make the list of those who change the world around them, but the "silly old fool" Elisha did. People who make a difference in their worlds are men and women of prophecy--people who know what God has said and simply take Him at His word. Their motto is, "God said it, I believe it, and that settles it!"

People of Piety

Her body literally convulsed with uncontrollable gut-wrenching sobs as tears flooded out in what seemed like cupfuls. As the tears continued to gush out, she somehow knew that they were not just coming from the ducts that surrounded her dark brown eyes; they were coming from somewhere much deeper inside her being. The thing that made these tears flow was not physical pain; therefore, these tears were not from her physical person. Her anguish was not from physical trauma but spiritual agony; therefore, her spiritual being was releasing its distress--and at the same time, ecstasy--through this soul-cleansing flood. Dissolved in each drop was a bit of her sordid past that was being washed out of her life. Each tear that ran down her cheek carried with it a particle of her past sins. Each drop of moisture washed to the surface more of her present adoration for the first man who had ever looked at her with true respect and acceptance rather than filthy, dehumanizing, abusive lust. Every tear glistened with the celebration of a future that promised that she actually could be somebody of value and worth. Those tears that poured out of her inner person that day seemed to be limitless because they flowed from an immeasurable emotional wellspring of repentance not only for her sinful actions but also for the image she had held of herself as something less than a carbon copy of the very image of God Himself. They sprang up from a boundless fountainhead of adoration for the one who made her know that she really was more than just a soulless machine for gratifying perverted lust. They erupted from an artesian gusher of hope deep inside her that had been plugged for so many years but had now been uncapped by the promise that she could actually go forward in life freed from her past of sin. Her tears were tears of rejoicing in the reality that her past had been eradicated and that she had been literally transformed through divine love. But more importantly, her tears were tears of virtuous worship for the only person who had ever invested genuine love in her.

In the same way that the tears seemed to wash the filth of the past out of her life, they dissolved the dirt and grime from the feet of the man over whom she wept that day. In the same way that these tears made her insides glisten, they cooled and refreshed the feet of the one at whose feet she knelt in incalculable love. In the way that the tears revitalized her soul with hope for the future, they prepared the feet of the one upon whom they fell for the next part of the journey He was about to undertake. Her tears were the tears of piety--the holy, godly worship that springs from our realization of the fact that God has forgiven us of our sins through divine, undeserved grace. This true, gut-level love for the one who has redeemed us through his indiscernibly sacrificial love must be the motivating force of the life of anyone who will truly make a difference in the world in which he lives.

In Daniel chapter nine, we can learn the story of a man whose piety in penitent prayer brought about a change not only in his own life but the life of a whole nation. The land had languished in desolation for seventy years, but now was time for restoration, and the key factor in bringing about that restoration lay in the pious faith of the prophet Daniel.

In verses 1-2, we see that there had to be a revelation of God's will in order for Daniel to act in confident faith.

> In the first year of Darius the son of Ahasuerus, of the seed of the Medes, which was made king over the realm of the Chaldeans; In the first year of his reign I Daniel understood by books the number of the years, whereof the word of the LORD came to Jeremiah the prophet, that he would accomplish seventy years in the desolations of Jerusalem.

Daniel understood from reading the book of Jeremiah (25:11, 12; 29:10) what God's plan was. It was only then that he began his prayer for the restoration of his nation.

He based his intercession on revelation he received from the Word of God--not just his own idea. He may have read this passage many times, but it was only after it became rhema to him that he could pray effectually about it.

Daniel's next ingredient was determination.

> And I set my face unto the Lord God, to seek by prayer and supplications, with fasting, and sackcloth, and ashes: (verse 3)

The first element in Daniel's intercession was that he set his face "unto the Lord." Here is a key to piety: we must remember that blessings come when we seek God, not the blessings themselves. We might say that the direction of our affection makes the connection.

During the sixteen years I spent working closely with Dr. Lester Sumrall, I had a number of occasions to be with him in times of private, personal prayer. The thing that was so powerful in those times of prayer was that I never heard him pray for television stations, airplanes, or buildings--though these things always came to his ministry in the right timing. His prayer was always, "I want to know You, Lord." This was the heart cry of a man who had already spent fifty years in the ministry!

Daniel next mentions that he sought the Lord through prayer and supplication, terms which can be interpreted as meaning communion and communication, connecting with God directly. Our answers come through dedication to the Lord, not by activities, programs, or techniques.

Finally, Daniel says that he interceded with fasting and sackcloth. Throughout the Bible, serious prayer is associated with fasting. This association has often led us to the misconception that fasting is a way to prove to God that we are serious about our requests. Actually, quite the opposite is true; through fasting, we prove to ourselves that we are serious about our requests. When we are more serious about seeking God than about fulfilling our human desires, we are on our way to a miracle answer. When we can strengthen our spirit man to the point that we can dominate our soulical and physical dimensions, we are entering into a realm of spiritual authority where we will see results from our prayers. Fasting is a propellant to our prayers. Many people feel that fasting is really a way to get God to do something that He has been reluctant to do previously. Their mentality is that if normal prayer doesn't get His attention, fasting will. At that point, we should ask ourselves, "Are we on a fast or a hunger strike?" If fasting is seen as a way to turn God's sympathy toward His poor, hungry children or as a way to prove our seriousness about our requests, then we really need to seriously rethink our relationship with God. The Bible teaches that it is faith that pleases God. (Hebrews 11:6) Jesus taught us to approach our Heavenly Father with the same kind of confidence that we approach our earthly fathers. (Matthew 7:9-11) With these ideas in mind, it is obvious that fasting must serve some function other than to be a way to persuade God to act. Actually, fasting should be a time of fellowship with God. It is not a time of outward mourning visible to our human neighbors. Instead, it is a time of inward seeking for the presence and favor of God.

> Moreover when ye fast, be not, as the hypocrites, of a sad countenance: for they disfigure their faces, that they may appear unto men to fast. Verily I say unto you, They have their reward. But thou, when thou fastest, anoint thine head, and wash thy face; That thou appear not unto men to fast, but unto thy Father which is in secret: and thy Father, which seeth in secret, shall reward thee openly. (Matthew 6:16-18)

When these hypocrites which Jesus mentioned woke up in the morning, they didn't bother washing their faces or combing their hair. They would go out into the street looking ragged as a sign that they were fasting. If this scripture were written in the twenty-first century, Jesus would have said, "Go ahead and take a nice hot shower in the morning, shave your face, and comb your hair." Jesus said that those who go around making a sign to people that they are fasting have their reward because everybody around them knows how miserable they are and admires them for it. Those people who fast secretly and use the time for fellowship with the Lord will be rewarded openly. Fasting brings the reward that you need from God into the open manifestation.

In verse four, Daniel makes his confession. He prayed his personal and individual heart feelings:

> And I prayed unto the LORD my God, and made my confession, and said, O Lord, the great and dreadful God, keeping the covenant and mercy to them that love him, and to them that keep his commandments;

Notice that his confession was not a recitation of his sins; rather, it was an affirmation of the truths he knew about God. First, he called on the infinite quality of God (O Lord). Like Isaiah who encountered God as high and lifted up with His train filling the temple (Isaiah 6:1), Daniel acknowledged God in His fullness. Next, he recited the covenant of God. This is exactly the approach which Jehoshaphat used in II Chronicles 20:6-9 when God answered so powerfully that He would fight the battle for His people and that they only needed to stand still and see His deliverance from the attack of the combined armies of Ammon, Moab, and Mount Seir. Next, Daniel called upon God as "my God," not just "God." It is of earth-changing significance when we recognize the personal relationship we have with God. No matter how much we acknowledge His omnipotence, if we don't recognize that He is in a personal relationship with us and is, therefore, willing to act on our behalf, we will not be able to appropriate that omnipotent power for our situation. A great example of this principle is found in I Samuel chapter seventeen when David stepped forward to fight against Goliath. For forty days, the entire army had cowered before the threats of the giant, yet David boldly stepped forward to take on the over-sized challenge. Why? Notice that throughout the chapter the army is continually referred to as "the army of Israel" and "the men of Saul." It is only David who sees himself as a member of the "army of the living God." That personal relationship with God gave the little shepherd boy a confidence that none of the trained soldiers could muster.

Finally, Daniel called on the mercy (benevolent generosity) of God. Even though he recognized that it was undeserved, the prophet could confidently petition God for grace. The life of Hosea, another of Israel's prophets, paints a dramatic picture of this undeserved benevolence of our God when he unwaveringly committed himself to his wife Gomer even though she sold herself in unfaithfulness and harlotry.

> And I will betroth thee unto me for ever; yea,
> I will betroth thee unto me in righteousness,
> and in judgment, and in lovingkindness, and
> in mercies. I will even betroth thee unto me
> in faithfulness: and thou shalt know the
> LORD. (Hosea 2:19-20)

In verse five, Daniel made a national confession for his people even though they had not personally repented. Unlike his personal confession, this one was a confession of sinfulness rather than a profession of one's position in God as Daniel had prayed in the previous verse.

> We have sinned, and have committed
> iniquity, and have done wickedly, and have
> rebelled, even by departing from thy
> precepts and from thy judgments:

The prophet listed six different levels of wrongdoing of his people. First, he mentions sin which could be literally translated as missing the mark. The imagery here is of an archer shooting an arrow. He seldom hits the bull's-eye and may even miss the entire target on occasion. There is not element of willfulness in missing the target; in fact, the archer is very purposefully trying to hit the bull's-eye. It is just his lack of ability that keeps him from scoring perfectly with every arrow. So it is with the majority of our shortcomings. Even though we try to do right, we fail simply because we are humans and are incapable of measuring up to God's standards.

Next, the prophet prayed for the people's iniquity, which is the inborn law of sin and death (Psalms 51:5) which works in all of us to keep us from living up to God's standards. Paul described the bondage of the iniquitous law of sin and death in Romans chapter seven when he said that even though he determined to do right he always wound up failing and when he determined not to do wrong he wound up doing so anyway. He summed up his situation with the desperate plea:

> O wretched man that I am! Who can deliver me from this body of death?
> (Romans 7:24)

Wickedness was Daniel's third category. By this term, he is referring to human immorality, our inability to withstand temptation. Next, he upped the ante by interceding for the people's rebellion, which is deliberate defiance of what we know is right. When he confessed that the nation had departed from God's precepts, he was acknowledging that they had deviated from the right path either by accident, ignorance, or even on purpose. Finally, he repented for the nation who had not hearkened to the prophets, denoting the people's deliberate disregard for divine authority.

In verses seven and eight, he used what might seem at first to be a rather unusual term to describe the people's condition, "confusion of face." This is a term which depicts the people as in a state of bewilderment. When people live in a constant and consistent state of sinfulness and disregard for divine authority, they become so confused as to the difference between right and wrong that God's evaluation is that they can't even tell their right hand from their left. (Jonah 4:11) "Confusion of face" seems a fitting evaluation of our present generation which spends more on pet food than on world missions, which can't seem to see the evil in ordaining homosexuals into the ministry, which uses more Christian broadcasting time talking about health products than ministering healing, which turns offering time into a get-rich-quick promotional, which requires parental permission to give a student an aspirin at school but will arrange an abortion without notifying the parents, which would rather pass out free condoms and needles than to tell teens to abstain from promiscuous sex and drug usage, which has criminalized any reference to Jesus during the celebration of His birthday, and which needs a constitutional amendment to help them define marriage as the union of one man and one woman.

In verses seven through nine, Daniel acknowledged that even the trespasses which might not have been deliberate sinfulness are of equal consequence with their defiant transgressions.

> O Lord, righteousness belongeth unto thee, but unto us confusion of faces, as at this day; to the men of Judah, and to the inhabitants of Jerusalem, and unto all Israel, that are near, and that are far off, through all the countries whither thou hast driven them, because of their trespass that they have trespassed against thee. O Lord, to us belongeth confusion of face, to our kings, to our princes, and to our fathers, because we have sinned against thee. To the Lord our God belong mercies and forgivenesses, though we have rebelled against him;

Daniel acknowledged in verses ten through twelve that restoration would come through learning to obey the voice of the Lord as well as His written Word. If we are to develop true piety, we must learn to walk in the spirit as well as the letter of the law.

> Neither have we obeyed the voice of the

> LORD our God, to walk in his laws, which he set before us by his servants the prophets. Yea, all Israel have transgressed thy law, even by departing, that they might not obey thy voice; therefore the curse is poured upon us, and the oath that is written in the law of Moses the servant of God, because we have sinned against him. And he hath confirmed his words, which he spake against us, and against our judges that judged us, by bringing upon us a great evil: for under the whole heaven hath not been done as hath been done upon Jerusalem.

In the next two verses, the prophet quickly recognized that until we turn away from sin and toward God, we will not be able to learn His truth which we have just determined in the previous verses to be the key to restoration.

> As it is written in the law of Moses, all this evil is come upon us: yet made we not our prayer before the LORD our God, that we might turn from our iniquities, and understand thy truth. Therefore hath the LORD watched upon the evil, and brought it upon us: for the LORD our God is righteous in all his works which he doeth: for we obeyed not his voice. And now, O Lord our God, that hast brought thy people forth out of the land of Egypt with a mighty hand, and hast gotten thee renown, as at this day; we have sinned, we have done wickedly.

In the following two verses, Daniel "pulled out his trump card." He appealed to God's own righteousness. Certainly, the sinfulness of man has disqualified him from making petitions to a holy God, and no amount of pleading on our part can convince the Almighty Sovereign to act. However, because of God's righteous nature, God is willing to act on behalf of His needy people. Daniel knew that this was the only "bargaining chip" he could use when pleading with God.

> O Lord, according to all thy righteousness, I beseech thee, let thine anger and thy fury be turned away from thy city Jerusalem, thy holy mountain: because for our sins, and for the iniquities of our fathers, Jerusalem and thy people are become a reproach to all that are about us. Now therefore, O our God, hear the prayer of thy servant, and his supplications, and cause thy face to shine upon thy sanctuary that is desolate.

He continued his appeal based on God's personal qualities in verses eighteen and nineteen.

> O my God, incline thine ear, and hear; open thine eyes, and behold our desolations, and the city which is called by thy name: for we do not present our supplications before thee for our righteousnesses, but for thy great mercies. O Lord, hear; O Lord, forgive; O Lord, hearken and do; defer not, for thine own sake, O my God: for thy city and thy people are called by thy name.

His point was that the real basis for God's intervention was that God wanted to act for His own name's sake. When He chose Abraham to receive His covenant, He did so in order to bless Abraham and establish him as a symbol so that the rest of the world could see what it meant to be in favor with God. He also established the people of Israel as a sign to show the nations what God can and will do with a people who serve Him. Isaiah said that they were "a light to the Gentiles." The Apostle Paul expressed the same idea when he said that we are ambassadors for Christ. No human government would ever select the uneducated, the ones who could not speak English, the ones with contagious diseases, the ones who didn't know how to dress properly, the insane, the ones with no social skills, or criminals to be their ambassadors. If we humans want to put our "best foot forward," God certainly wants to put forward a people who are healed (and not just healed, but overflowing with healing for others), saved (and not just saved, but overflowing with salvation for others), joyous (and not just joyous, but overflowing with joy to others), prosperous (and not just prosperous, but overflowing with prosperity to others)--in general, He wants a restored and blessed people. He wants them for His own reputation's sake!

Daniel's testimony in the following two verses confirmed that God is ready and willing to answer the prayers of a pious man when he prays fervently and effectually in alignment with God's will. Isaiah 65:24 declares that He will answer even before we call and that He will hear while we are still speaking. Matthew 6:8 emphasizes that He already knows what we need before we ask, and Luke 18:8 promises that He will answer speedily.

> And whiles I was speaking, and praying, and confessing my sin and the sin of my people Israel, and presenting my supplication before the LORD my God for the holy mountain of my God; Yea, whiles I was speaking in prayer, even the man Gabriel, whom I had seen in the vision at the beginning, being caused to fly swiftly, touched me about the time of the evening oblation.

God's answer came in verse twenty-two where He promised Daniel skill and understanding. We seem to always think that God should give us a physical answer; however, He often prefers to give us the supernatural ability to bring our own answer to pass. Peter, for example, was not handed a coin to pay his taxes; instead, he was given a divine blessing upon his fishing talent so that he was able to catch the one fish which was carrying a coin around in its mouth. (Matthew 17:24-27) We often pray for a spiritual anointing, but God often answers that He wants to equip us in the physical and soulical as well as in the spiritual realms. The world will not be won to Christ through our intelligence and presentation, but it certainly will not be won without them.

> And he informed me, and talked with me, and said, O Daniel, I am now come forth to give thee skill and understanding.

In the last verse related to Daniel's intercession, the Lord reconfirmed that whatever He does is because of His love--not even because Daniel followed a formula which included all the principles in the prayer. It is because we are beloved that we get our answer.

> At the beginning of thy supplications the commandment came forth, and I am come to shew thee; for thou art greatly beloved: therefore understand the matter, and consider the vision.

If we study the historical timing of this prayer, we'll see that at the exact time when Daniel prayed, the Lord started moving upon the king of Persia to allow the Jews to return to Jerusalem and rebuild the temple! The prayer of a man of piety brought about God's immediate response and made a difference in a seventy-year-old problem.

People Who Understand Prosperity

He wondered if his face had betrayed him. Did it reflect the horror that gripped his heart when he heard the teacher's reply to his question? Although his question was genuine, he couldn't say that his motive had been totally pure. When he asked the teacher what he needed to do to enter the kingdom, he totally expected the reply to be a reassuring commendation of all his good works and charitable acts. Instead, the teacher's response was that he would have to sell everything he owned and give the proceeds to the poor! At that verdict, our friend was sure that his face must have turned as white as his knuckles were as he grasped tightly to his fortune. Each day for the rest of his life, that incident haunted him. Had he missed the opportunity of a lifetime--no, not just a lifetime, the opportunity of an eternity? Every time he saw the beggars who sat on the corner just outside the shop where his wife bought all her extravagant garments, his mind raced back to that one brief encounter. When he saw the loose lifestyle that his son had adopted, he wondered how long his hard-earned fortune would remain after his death. Would it be lost in the gambling hall while so many desperate people who shiver in the cold and go hungry could have received so much more than the empty thrill the boy would enjoy as he wagered away his inheritance? But most of all, the nagging query that would never leave his mind was whether he had truly traded the riches of the kingdom of heaven for the fool's gold of this life. He had the opportunity to make a difference in his world, but he chose not to in favor of gasping on to his prosperity. People who make a difference are those who understand godly prosperity.

The Apostle Paul wrote to the Corinthian church that God was able to make all grace abound toward them so that they would always have all sufficiency in all things and that they would abound to every good work. (II Corinthians 9:8) This passage is in the context of the offering he was receiving for the saints in Jerusalem who had been devastated by the famine which ravaged Palestine. The Apostle was encouraging them to liberally contribute to the cause with the assurance that God would see to it that they would have sufficiency, or enough to cover all their own personal needs and even adequate excess to give into every other worthwhile endeavor. Even a surface reading of this passage is encouraging and is certainly grounds to make us rejoice over the promised blessings we receive from the Lord. However, if we take a little time to look at the verse and analyze the wording from God's dictionary rather than relying on our own human definitions, we will see that the true meaning is a quantum leap beyond what first seems to appear on the page.

To grasp the meaning of the word "sufficiency" from God's perspective, we need to look back to the story of the building of the tabernacle. When Moses put out a call for donations of materials for the sanctuary, the people responded with such unexpected generosity that Moses had to command the people to stop giving because "the stuff they had was sufficient for all the work to make it, and too much" (Exodus 36:7) or "much more than enough." (verse 5) The same results came during Hezekiah's reformation when the priests declared that the people had brought in all that was needed and an abundance for storage. (II Chronicles 31:10) When the people of Samaria were so close to starvation that women were eating their own children, Elisha spoke into their desperate situation proclaiming that food would be available in abundance within twenty-four hours. In disbelief, one of the city officials proclaimed that it could not be so even if God were to open the windows of heaven. (II Kings 7:2) Amazingly, immeasurable supplies fell into their hands that next day as the windows of heaven were flung open. The final prophet of the Old Testament spoke of God's desire to open the windows of heaven--not just to the Samaritans, but to anyone who is willing to receive. He goes on to say that God will pour (or "empty" according to the original Hebrew wording) out a blessing that is beyond our capacity to receive. (Malachi 3:10) In other words, God's definition of "sufficient" is not "just enough"; it is "too much." Jesus affirmed this definition in Luke 6:38 when He instructed us, "Give, and it shall be given unto you; good measure, pressed down, and shaken together, and running over, shall men give into your bosom. For with the same measure that ye mete withal it shall be measured to you again."

      A couple stories from the Old Testament and a couple illustrations from the New may help drive home the point. In I Kings chapter seventeen, we find the story of a widow in Zarephath who was preparing the last meal before she and her son were destined to starve to death. Just as she was collecting a few sticks to start her last cook fire, the prophet Elijah showed up asking for a meal. After hearing her objections based on her distressed state, the prophet promised that God would multiply her oil and meal for the duration of the drought. Making enough food each day to feed her, the lad, and the man of God would have been sufficiency according to human standards; however, according to verse fifteen, there was enough to feed a whole household in addition to the three of them. In chapter four of II Kings, we read another story about another widow, another prophet, and another miraculous multiplication of oil. This time, the widow came to Elisha begging for help because her two sons were to be taken as indentured servants to pay off her deceased husband's debts. Elisha's response was that God was going to multiply the one bottle of oil she had so that she could sell it and pay the debt. The human definition of "sufficiency" would have caused the oil to have stopped multiplying as soon as the budget was met, but the divine definition determined that the miracle continue until there was enough for her and her children--possibly several others in addition to the two boys who were in trouble--to live on! (verse 7)

      One additional story from the Old Testament tells us about the lives of two widows in one family--Naomi and her daughter-in-law Ruth. Ruth went out to glean in the fields in hopes of finding enough overlooked grain to sustain the pair. In her evaluation, a few handfuls of barley would have been enough; but from God's vantage point, she was to get not only something to eat but a husband and the whole barley field!

In the New Testament, we read of two different occasions when Jesus miraculously multiplied bread and fish to feed the hungry multitudes who came to hear Him preach. On one occasion, five loaves fed five thousand men plus an unnumbered throng of women and children. At the other feast, seven loaves fed four thousand men plus the accompanying women and children. Human economics would have had the multiplication stop when all the hungry mouths were fed, but heavenly mathematics had the miracle continue until there were twelve baskets in excess at one banquet and seven at the other. (Mark 8:19-20)

As with any truth, it is important to remember that a misapplied truth can be just as devastating as a deliberately applied lie. If we misappropriate the principle and misread the directions to make it sound as if honoring and obeying the scriptures is the means to success and prosperity, we have gotten the cart before the horse, as the old expression would put it. The truth is that our goal should be to live by the scriptural truths regardless of any resulting benefits. These blessings are merely the byproducts of a life that pleases the Lord and values His Word. Jesus specifically warned us that a focus on the things God gives rather than the Giver Himself is greed and covetousness--a violation of the tenth commandment.

> And he said unto them, Take heed, and beware of covetousness: for a man's life consisteth not in the abundance of the things which he possesseth. (Luke 12:15)

A newsman interviewing one of America's wealthiest businessmen asked the question, "How much will be enough?" The tycoon responded with a sheepish little grin,

"Just a little bit more." One indicator of greed is that it is never satisfied; enough is never enough. Although we have already seen that God never feels that He has given us enough and continues to bless more abundantly, He does not expect us to develop a "black hole" mentality that can never be filled.

> Yea, they are greedy dogs which can never have enough, and they are shepherds that cannot understand [The original Hebrew wording reads, "Don't know how to be satisfied."]: they all look to their own way, every one for his gain, from his quarter. (Isaiah 56:11)
>
> He that loveth silver shall not be satisfied with silver; nor he that loveth abundance with increase: this is also vanity. (Ecclesiastes 5:10)
>
> For they shall eat, and not have enough: they shall commit whoredom, and shall not increase: because they have left off to take heed to the LORD. (Hosea 4:10)
>
> The sleep of a labouring man is sweet, whether he eat little or much: but the abundance of the rich will not suffer him to sleep. (Ecclesiastes 5:12)

The citizens of Jerusalem had this problem because they were so consumed with their own needs that they failed to take care of their responsibilities concerning the temple. Haggai wrote, "Ye have sown much, and bring in little; ye eat, but ye have not enough; ye drink, but ye are not filled with drink; ye clothe you, but there is none warm; and he that earneth wages earneth wages to put it into a bag with holes." (Haggai 1:6) It was only after they turned their attention away from themselves and dedicated themselves and their resources to the Lord's work that they were able to enjoy true sufficiency.

Consider now from this day and upward,

> from the four and twentieth day of the ninth month, even from the day that the foundation of the LORD'S temple was laid, consider it. Is the seed yet in the barn? yea, as yet the vine, and the fig tree, and the pomegranate, and the olive tree, hath not brought forth: from this day will I bless you. (Haggai 2:18-19)

Another indicator is that we begin to think that our abundance is our own, not necessarily the blessing of God.

> Not that we are sufficient of ourselves to think any thing as of ourselves; but our sufficiency is of God. (II Corinthians 3:5)

> Charge them that are rich in this world, that they be not highminded, nor trust in uncertain riches, but in the living God, who giveth us richly all things to enjoy. (I Timothy 6:17)

> Lo, this is the man that made not God his strength; but trusted in the abundance of his riches, and strengthened himself in his wickedness. (Psalms 52:7)

The truly blessed man in one who can recognize God's blessing in every area of his life without letting these blessings overwhelm him. Solomon, possibly one of the wealthiest men to have ever lived on Planet Earth, made this reasonable summation concerning prosperity:

> Hast thou found honey? eat so much as is sufficient for thee, lest thou be filled therewith, and vomit it. (Proverbs 25:16)

> Two things have I required of thee; deny me them not before I die: Remove far from me vanity and lies: give me neither poverty nor riches; feed me with food convenient for me: Lest I be full, and deny thee, and say, Who is the LORD? or lest I be poor, and steal, and take the name of my God in vain.

(Proverbs 30:7-9)

The Apostle Paul was able to consider himself to be abounding even while yet a prisoner because his true abundance was in the heart more than in his wallet.

> But I have all, and abound: I am full, having received of Epaphroditus the things which were sent from you, an odour of a sweet smell, a sacrifice acceptable, wellpleasing to God. (Philippians 4:18)

This is a powerful lesson to add to anything else we have learned about God's sufficiency: let Him be sufficient in His own way. For an example we can turn to the Old Testament stories of the prophets Elisha and Elijah. Both of these men of God faced similar problems and received supernatural answers from God proving that He is all sufficient; however, the two solutions proved that the same Lord could solve the same problems without being forced into a box. After Elijah left the Brook Cherith, he came to Zarephath where the Lord directed him to the widow who was to support him throughout the rest of the drought. As we have already learned, the miraculous provision for the widow came from a single bottle of oil which multiplied daily until the famine ended. Elijah's protégée, Elisha, also had a miraculous provision for a widow with a single bottle of oil. This time, the oil multiplied instantaneously and became a one-time provision to fill the immediate lack with sufficiency for all future need. Two widows with single bottles of oil trusted the same God who intervened in both of their situations by supernaturally multiplying the oil; one experienced a daily miracle while the other received an all-at-once provision. God's sufficiency can come in any way He chooses to provide it--either with barns being filled with plenty and presses bursting out with new wine (Proverbs 3:10) or with bread sufficient for our daily needs (Matthew 6:11); but either way, it is His sufficiency!

Another barrier we must get beyond is the mentality that sufficiency is always material. Just take a moment to remember the story of Gideon. To him, the thirty-two thousand soldiers who responded to his first call was sufficiency. God, however, saw that the majority of them were unprepared and scared. When the number was pared down, Gideon reluctantly re-adjusted his estimation of sufficiency to only ten thousand men. To Gideon's utter amazement, the Lord again announced that the men were too many. It was only when the troops were culled to three hundred that Gideon learned God's definition of "sufficiency." The disciples had to learn the same lesson and break through the same barrier in John chapter six when Jesus asked them to feed the hungry multitude. Phillip's immediate response was to count the pennies in the coffer because he was clinging to the human definition of "enough." His evaluation was that two hundred pennies was not enough to feed the crowd. Before we too quickly agree with him, we should stop to calculate exactly how much money he was talking about. From one of Jesus' parables, we learn that a penny was an acceptable wage for a day of labor. Using this as a basis, we can calculate that the sum of money he was talking about was the pre-tax income of an average worker for a period of forty weeks, or ten months, not just small pocket change. Andrew, on the other hand, brought out a handful of fish and loaves and asked what Jesus could do with his little offering. You see, he had come to understand the divine definition of "sufficiency"--"Little is much when God is in it." To emphasize the point, Jesus made sure that there was more left over after the people had eaten than there had been to start with!

God's view of prosperity is based more on resourcefulness that on resources. For examples we can look at the churches addressed in the book of Revelation. To the church at Laodicea, the Lord says, "Because thou sayest, I am rich, and increased with goods, and have need of nothing; and knowest not that thou art wretched, and miserable, and poor, and blind, and naked: I counsel thee to buy of me gold tried in the fire, that thou mayest be rich; and white raiment, that thou mayest be clothed, and that the shame of thy nakedness do not appear; and anoint thine eyes with eyesalve, that thou mayest see." (Revelation 3:17-18) They apparently had resources but lacked the true prosperity of God necessary for their spiritual and physical wellbeing. The church at Smyrna is addressed as "rich" in the midst of their poverty. (Revelation 2:9) What they lacked in material resources was more than compensated for in their spiritual resourcefulness. Like Peter when he met the lame man at the Beautiful Gate, these believers knew that even though they didn't have silver and gold, there was something that they did have in and through the name of Jesus that was of much more value and effectiveness.

    The unfortunate reality is that it is all too easy to forget even after we have learned the truth about God's sufficiency in our lives. King David boasted in Psalms 20:7, "Some trust in chariots, and some in horses: but we will remember the name of the LORD our God," declaring that his confidence was not in the strength of his army, but in the sufficiency of his God. However, near the end of his reign, David directed his commander to take a census of all available fighting men. Joab resisted the order, citing the Lord's sufficiency on behalf of His people, but the king insisted and prevailed--a deliberate action which resulted in God's anger and judgment. It seems likely that God's displeasure was not so much a result of the fact that David wanted to know the number of warriors he had available as it was the fact that the king had fallen from a previous position of faith and trust in God.

    My prayer is that we remain in His grace so that we can truly know His divine prosperity.

> And God is able to make all grace abound toward you; that ye, always having all sufficiency in all things, may abound to every good work: (II Corinthians 9:8)

The whole purpose of prosperity is to have ample

resources to properly care for yourself and family and have extra to make a difference in others' lives. The friend we met at the beginning of this section had plenty of money but he fell far short of being prosperous because he was unwilling to use what was in his hand to make a difference in the lives of others.

People of Praise

Had he lived a couple millennia later, I'm sure that he would have felt like the emperor parading down the street in his new clothes which actually turned out to be his birthday suit. God was asking the king to stand up against three unified armies and expect to see the victory by simply having the praise band strike up a tune. Certainly Jehoshaphat felt just as exposed and vulnerable as Hans Christian Andersen's character when he realized that the tailor had stolen the "very shirt off of his back"--and a whole lot more! How in the world would a lively chorus of "This is the Day" make a difference? Certainly, it was about to be the day for him! But regardless of the logic, the king stepped forward and made the decree that the praisers were to take the lead. Suddenly, the whole world seemed to turn around as his enemies took up their weapons and began to attack one another rather than his army! By the end of the day, there was no opponent standing but the battlefield was littered with loot and booty--in fact, so much that it took his men three days to collect it all!

Praise is actually a form of prayer and spiritual warfare that helps us make a difference in the world around us. The Bible tells us that it is with thanksgiving that we are able to enter into His gates and that we can enter into His courts with praise. One of the major keys to a successful Christian life is an attitude of gratitude. If we look only a little, we can always find something for which to be thankful and to express our gratitude. A story is told about a nursing home employee who really knew and applied this principle. One night there was a terrible ice storm, but the next morning she reported to work as promptly as ever. Surprised to see her, her supervisor asked how she had made it. "I live only two blocks away," she said, "so I just crawled on my hands and knees, and here I am! I'm so thankful." "Just what is there about crawling up a hill on your hands and knees, through ice and snow, at six o'clock in the morning that would make you so thankful?" the supervisor asked. Removing her wet coat, she replied, "It was dark--no one could see me!"

In our lives, there is always something we can be thankful for and something that we can praise God for, no matter what the situation may be. The Bible enjoins us to verbalize our praise to God in a joyful noise. Even if our praises may not do much for others, God loves them and welcomes them. A student came with a pressing problem, "The past couple days I've been tempted by lustful sexual thoughts. This is the first real problem I've had since receiving the baptism of the Holy Spirit about four months ago. What can I do?" My answer was "Praise the Lord." I meant that as something to actually do. A lot of times we just say, "Praise the Lord" as a Christian cliché, but this time I meant it as an act to take in overcoming temptation. Then I reminded him of some of the principles concerning James' directions to count it all joy when we are tempted and Paul's admonition to glory in tribulations.

> My brethren, count it all joy when you fall into divers temptations knowing this that the trying of your faith worketh patience but let patience have her perfect work that ye may be perfect and entire wanting nothing. (James 1:2)
>
> And not only so, but we glory in tribulations also: knowing that tribulation worketh patience; And patience, experience; and experience, hope: (Romans 5:2:4)

From these verses, it is easy to see that these great apostles didn't count temptation and troubles as occasions for discouragement. Rather, temptation was an occasion for praising the Lord. Joy and rejoicing were their responses when Satan tried to get them down. They knew that they needed strength and they must have remembered that Nehemiah had said that "the joy of the Lord is your strength." Paul had proved that joy rather than discouragement was the better response to trouble when he and Silas were in the Philippian jail. (Acts 16:24-26) They had been beaten, imprisoned, and held in chains. At midnight, when everything was the darkest, they were singing and praising God. Through their praises, an earthquake delivered them from the jail. These apostles could rejoice and praise God through their troubles because they saw that the final result of all soulical temptation and physical tribulation is a stronger spiritual character. James claimed that the final result was "wanting nothing," and Paul saw that it was "having nothing to make you ashamed."

Praising God is an absolute necessity to being an overcomer. Praise is an actual form of warfare. When we praise God, we establish a place for the Lord to live. "The Lord inhabits the praises of his people." (Psalm 22:3) Where He is there is joy. "In the presence of the Lord there is fulness of joy." (Psalm 16:11) That joy will produce strength. "The joy of the Lord is our strength." (Nehemiah 8:10) From the strength that we receive from the Lord as a result of the joy, we know that we can "do all things through Christ Jesus who strengthens me." (Philippians 4:12) Our praise establishes the presence, which brings the joy, which produces the strength with the end result that we are victorious in all things. Praise warfare is a very important key that we must have. We must go into spiritual warfare with an attitude of total victory. Prayer is the propelling force to get us through. Praise warfare establishes strength in our lives.

Second Chronicles chapter twenty tells the story of Jehoshaphat, who actually had the garments of praise (Isaiah 61:3) rather than the emperor's faux attire. When he was far outnumbered as the armies of the enemies were approaching, Jehoshaphat declared a fast and sought the Lord for His intervention. The Lord answered, "Do not be afraid nor dismayed because of this great multitude for the battle is not yours but God's...You will not need to fight in this battle. Position yourselves, stand still and see the salvation of the Lord who is with you." Then all the people of Israel worshiped the Lord. Praise and worship are the important elements that won the victory for Jehoshaphat.

Victory can also be the result of our praise. Jehoshaphat did indeed have his army dressed in battle array, ready for combat. Remember that Paul tells us to take on the whole armor of God. We can't just act like there isn't a battle. We need to get dressed for the battle even though we know that God will do the fighting. We must equip ourselves with our battle gear. When Jehoshaphat's army began to sing and praise, the Lord sent ambushes against the people of Ammon, Moab, and Mount Seir who had come against Judah. Ammon and Moab got confused and started fighting the army of Mount Seir; they then fought against themselves until they destroyed one another. It took Jehoshaphat three days to carry off all the spoils of war. On the fourth day, they worshiped God and returned to Jerusalem "with joy for the Lord had made them to rejoice over their enemies." (verse 27)

James tells us to "count it all joy," not because we are to have the struggle but because we have the promise that we will come out from the struggle stronger than when we went in. When Jehoshaphat's army went in to fight the battle, they did not have that bounty of loot and booty in their hands. They came into the battle with a concern in their soulical man. They sought God. When they used their praise to propel their spiritual weapons, they went into spiritual battle. Instead of losing their houses, land, and families, they returned home with wagonloads of goods. They came back better than when they went out to fight. James tells us that when we come to a temptation or trial we should face it with rejoicing because we realize that on the other side we will be better off for having gone through it. He assures us that the end result will be that we are not ashamed. Jehoshaphat came back full of rejoicing because not only had their enemy been defeated, but they also came back to Jerusalem with great wealth. He made a difference through praise.

People with Positive Confessions

She was little more than a blur flashing before their eyes as she raced past at breakneck speed. Her hair stood almost straight out in the wind behind her as her donkey broke almost every record time ever clocked for his species. Before the cloud of dust she had kicked up could settle, the Shunammite woman disappeared into the distance. What could have been so important that she hurried so? Was there some sort of emergency that demanded more than immediate attention? At both ends of her journey, she was asked the same challenging questions. When she asked her husband to have a young man bring her the donkey for her trip, he questioned, "Why are you going to visit the prophet today? It is not a holiday nor the sabbath." Her answer was three simple words, "It is well." (II Kings 4:23) When she got within eyesight of the prophet, he was troubled with the apparent urgency of her visit and sent his servant to meet her and inquire, "Is it well with you? Is it well with your husband? Is it well with your child?" Again she replied with the same three simple words, "It is well." (verse 26) However, when she finally reached the prophet, she bared her soul and told him the tragic news--her son was dead! What kind of woman must this lady have been to have not even told her husband that his own son was lying dead inside the house? Was she demented, deranged, disoriented, or deceived? Was she some sort of a religious fanatic involved in some cultish "name it, claim it, frame it" doctrine? Was she deceived into believing that if she denied the facts that they would just disappear and go away? No! She was an intelligent woman with standing in society and respect before people in the highest places. (II Kings 8:5-6) She was not some off-the-wall fanatic who believed in rejecting reality; on the contrary, she clearly acknowledged the facts but was able to recognize a higher level of reality than many people could have discerned. She clearly saw the fact that her son was dead--and she had no problem admitting it to the prophet. However, she also understood that the boy had been given to her as a gift from God and she understood enough of the nature of God to know that He would not tantalize her with a "carrot on a stick" by giving her a gift and then snatching it away before she had the opportunity to enjoy its blessings. She understood that He is a God whose blessing makes us rich and that He never adds sorrow with them. (Proverbs 10:22) Because she knew and understood this higher level of reality, she could make the positive confession, "It is well"! She was not denying any facts or reality, she was simply confessing the facts and realities that she understood from her insight into a higher level of reality than that which most people around her--including her husband and the prophet's servant--can perceive.

So why was she in such a hurry to get to the prophet? She apparently also understood a couple other spiritual principles: the power of the tongue and the power of agreement. Since life and death are both in the power of the tongue (Proverbs 18:21), she needed to deal with the son's death before others had occasion to begin to make too many negative statements. Had she allowed her husband to have known about the child's condition, he would have filled the community with the report of the boy's demise and everyone would soon be speaking words of death into the situation. Had she told Gehazi what had happened to the boy, he would have joined in with the negative report. Apparently she knew that there was only one living human who would see into the divine realm of reality and understand the facts like she did. She had to get to him as soon as possible before someone else stumbled upon the corpse and began to speak forth words of death into the situation. She seemed to realize that if she could get to the prophet, he would agree with her and exponentially raise the power of her positive confession. (Deuteronomy 32:30) Time was of the essence for her, not because she was running from the boy's death but because she was running toward his resurrection! Her positive confession that all was well even when the evidence indicated otherwise made the life-and-death difference for her son!

A number of years ago, I was in a biking accident which left me with a broken shoulder blade. When my wife took me to the emergency room for X-rays to determine the extent of the injury, I found it almost impossible to get out of the car because my right arm was hanging uselessly at my side. When someone in the parking lot noticed my struggle and offered to help, I refused with the words, "I'm fine." When I finally did get out of the car, I laughed to myself at the scene--a man with his hand and arm dangling totally uselessly as he attempted the simple task of getting out of a car and closing the door behind himself--all the while declaring that he was fine! I'm sure that it was a sight similar to the Shunammite woman's feverish donkey ride. But the truth of the matter was that I really was fine. I refused to allow the physical evidence to override the spiritual promises that I base my life on--and within a couple weeks the arm was miraculously healed and I was off on a long-planned backpacking trip to Europe!!

People who want to make a difference must learn to make positive confessions about the situations and people they encounter. These confessions must be based on the scriptural promises rather than the present evidence. When we see people and situations as God sees them and we agree with His assessment of the matter, we will make a godly difference!

People Who Face Persecution

You could read his body like a book. It was a journal that chronicled his life. His back was a veritable roadmap connecting almost every major city in Israel, Turkey, Greece, and Italy with scars from beatings he had received in each place. Five different lashings of thirty-nine stripes each had left potholes from the violence of the whips as they literally snatched chunks of tissue from his torso. Ribbons of scar tissue testified to the lesions caused as the whips tore through his flesh. The hesitancy in his gait testified of the three times he had been clubbed. The bald patches on his chest where the skin had been rubbed so raw that no chest hair would grow were the mementoes of the three different times he had spent whole days and nights desperately clinging to pieces of drift wood to keep from drowning after having been shipwrecked in the Mediterranean. Jagged claw marks on his forearms and the scar that ran dangerously close to his jugular vein were evidences of his struggle with wild beasts in Ephesus. The calluses around his wrists and ankles were the signatures left by the chains and shackles from almost every prison between Jerusalem and Rome. The two companion puncture wounds on the inside of his arm were a souvenir left behind by a venomous serpent on the island of Malta. The contusions on the side of his face were a witness to the day he was stoned and left for dead in Lystra. Yet, as he ran his left hand across this ledger of injuries, he picked up a pen and parchment in his right hand and scratched out the memorable words, "Our light affliction, which is but for a moment, worketh for us a far more exceeding and eternal weight of glory." (II Corinthians 4:17) How could it be? Why would the Apostle Paul say such a thing? Simply because he knew that what he had endured was a key element in making a difference.

I was struggling with the decision as to whether to include this last "P" in the list of qualities that define men and women who make a difference when I had one of those divine coincidences that we can only define as "God appointments." The keynote speaker at a missions conference I was attending gave a list of the characteristics of the pioneer missionaries who become successful church planters. At the very bottom of his list was one final entry which he said he had struggled over including. He had put it on and then taken it off and then re-added it. Finally, he decided that even though it was not a universal characteristic, it was so prevalent that it deserved to be listed. So it made it on his list and on mine--persecution. People who make a difference must be ready to face and endure persecution even it may not actually befall them.

Persecution is prophetically part of the church's destiny. Jesus listed persecution right along with the earthquakes, wars, and famines as a sign of the last days.

> And Jesus went out, and departed from the temple: and his disciples came to him for to shew him the buildings of the temple. And Jesus said unto them, See ye not all these things? Verily I say unto you, There shall not be left here one stone upon another, that shall not be thrown down. And as he sat upon the mount of Olives, the disciples came unto him privately, saying, Tell us, when shall these things be? and what shall be the sign of thy coming, and of the end of the world? And Jesus answered and said unto them, Take heed that no man deceive you. For many shall come in my name, saying, I am Christ; and shall deceive many. And ye shall hear of wars and rumors of wars: see that ye be not troubled: for all these things must come to pass, but the end is not yet. For nation shall rise against nation, and kingdom against kingdom: and there shall be famines, and pestilences, and earthquakes, in diverse places. All these are the beginning of sorrows. <u>Then shall</u>

> they deliver you up to be afflicted, and shall kill you: and ye shall be hated of all nations for my name's sake. And then shall many be offended, and shall betray one another, and shall hate one another. And many false prophets shall rise, and shall deceive many. And because iniquity shall abound, the love of many shall wax cold. But he that shall endure unto the end, the same shall be saved. And this gospel of the kingdom shall be preached in all the world for a witness unto all nations; and then shall the end come. (Matthew 24:1-14)

Jesus reemphasized the prophecy of coming suffering for Christians as part of His last instructions to His disciples.

> These things have I spoken unto you, that ye should not be offended. They shall put you out of the synagogues: yea, the time cometh, that whosoever killeth you will think that he doeth God service. And these things will they do unto you, because they have not known the Father, nor me. If the world hate you, ye know that it hated me before it hated you. If ye were of the world, the world would love his own: but because ye are not of the world, but I have chosen you out of the world, therefore the world hateth you. Remember the word that I said unto you, The servant is not greater than his lord. If they have persecuted me, they will also persecute you; if they have kept my saying, they will keep yours also. But all these things will they do unto you for my name's sake, because they know not him that sent me. If I had not come and spoken unto them, they had not had sin: but now they have no cloak for their sin. He that

hateth me hateth my Father also. If I had not done among them the works which none other man did, they had not had sin: but now have they both seen and hated both me and my Father. But this cometh to pass, that the word might be fulfilled that is written in their law, They hated me without a cause. (John 15:1-3, 18-25)

As I read these words from our Master, I am convinced that Jesus is talking about a universal persecution which will engulf the church world-wide. The church of God has always known persecution--remember the Christians versus the lions. I once saw a cartoon depicting a modern man watching a television program about the early Christians being fed to the lions in the Roman amphitheater. The caption read, "Christianity didn't used to be a spectator sport." A following line added, "It still isn't." The truth is that today the Christian faith is experiencing more widespread attacks than at any other time in history. More Christians were slaughtered in the twentieth century than the total causalities of World War I, World War II, the Vietnam War, and the Korean War combined! Yet, most of us have no concept that over two hundred million of our Christian brothers and sisters around the world live under severe conditions of oppression and persecution. Most of us have no realization of what it means that these believers live under a constant threat of imprisonment, torture, slavery, and even death. Most of us are totally foreign to the fact that blood is being spilled every day on behalf of the gospel which we so nonchalantly take as a given in our lives. Thousands of martyrs are being slaughtered in countries which have Muslim, Buddhist, Hindu, or other anti-Christian controlled governments. Religious fanaticism is causing problems for Christians in many parts of the world. "Destroy all Christian churches today!" scream typical headlines in prominent Hindu newspapers. Some papers have openly called for a campaign of genocide against non-Hindus who refuse to deny Jesus Christ and convert to Hinduism. Death threats are common both in print and on the field. The Buddhist controlled governments of some Asian countries have been working on exterminating entire tribes of hundreds of thousands of people just because they are predominately Christians. Modern helicopter gun ships and armies have been used in some areas to exterminate entire population regions of Christians. One Western observer witnessed a gun ship using a rapid fire 50-mm cannon stirring up a rage of dust behind a fleeing six-year-old boy. The deadly projectiles caught up with their target as a pastor ran to help the terrified boy. Both were decimated, as well as hundreds of others trying to flee the village from the Moslem armies. The women and young girls were then herded away to be sold as sex slaves to Moslem men.

Several years ago, a little insert encouraging us to pray for the persecuted church was enclosed in our church bulletin. One startling sentence was emblazoned into my heart as I took the few minutes necessary to read the flyer: "By the time you finish reading this page, another brother or sister will have given his or her life for the faith." One believer is martyred every three and a half minutes. That means that while most churches are making their announcements, one of our brothers has been announced at the Pearly Gates as a new arrival through martyrdom; while we sing one worship song, one of our sisters has performed the ultimate act of worship; in the time it takes most churches to receive the offering, two of our brothers or sisters have made the most acceptable offering possible. When we realize the suffering that our brothers and sisters are enduring, the Holy Spirit will begin to motivate us to pray as He did Bob Pierce, the founder of World Vision, "Let my heart be broken by the things that break the heart of God." Jesus Himself interceded for Peter when He realized that the disciple was headed into a trying ordeal.

And the Lord said, Simon, Simon, behold,

> Satan hath desired to have you, that he may sift you as wheat: But I have prayed for thee, that thy faith fail not: and when thou art converted, strengthen thy brethren. (Luke 22:31-32)

When I first began to study this topic, I resisted by telling the Lord that I was a "good news" preacher and did not want to bring bad news to the people I so dearly love. He reminded me that if I teach only from the Bible, I couldn't be preaching bad news because the word "gospel" itself literally means "good news"! The bad news is that the Bible predicts that the church will experience universal persecution in the these last days. The good news is that God has made a provision for us in this persecution!

Jesus gave us at least three great directives concerning how we are to respond to persecution. The first is found in Matthew 5:11-12.

> Blessed are ye, when men shall revile you, and persecute you, and shall say all manner of evil against you falsely, for my sake. Rejoice and be exceedingly glad: for great is your reward in heaven: for so persecuted they the prophets which were before you.

There are two great principles to learn from this passage. The first one is that we must look at persecution positively. Jesus said that we are blessed when we are persecuted. We are all eager for God's blessings--thinking of money, good health, nice homes, and happy families. How many of us have virtually memorized the first portion of Deuteronomy twenty-eight as we have so frequently quoted the litany of blessings listed there? But being persecuted isn't exactly on that list! Jesus goes on to say that this persecution is actually a reason to celebrate and rejoice! Perhaps a little look at the book of Hebrews might give us an insight into how we can actually rejoice when facing persecution. In the great "roll call of faith" in chapter eleven, those who had to endure suffering and loss were no less men of faith than those who were listed as ones who saw miraculous deliverances. In Hebrews 11:32-40 we learn something about the differences between them. Notice that some of them were delivered <u>from</u> their persecution. This was a deliverance of the body.

> And what shall I more say? for the time would fail me to tell of Gedeon, and of Barak, and of Samson, and of Jephthae; of David also, and Samuel, and of the prophets: Who through faith subdued kingdoms, wrought righteousness, obtained promises, stopped the mouths of lions, Quenched the violence of fire, escaped the edge of the sword. (verses 32-34a)

Others were delivered <u>in</u> their persecution. This deliverance was of the soul.

> out of weakness were made strong, waxed valiant in fight, turned to flight the armies of the aliens. Women received their dead raised to life again. (verses 34b-35a)

Still others were delivered <u>through</u> their persecution. These experienced deliverance in the spirit.

> and others were tortured, not accepting deliverance; that they might obtain a better resurrection: And others had trial of cruel mockings and scourgings, yea, moreover of bonds and imprisonment: They were stoned, they were sawn asunder, were tempted, were slain with the sword: they wandered about in sheepskins and goatskins; being destitute, afflicted, tormented; (Of whom the world was not worthy) they wandered in deserts, and in mountains, and in dens and caves of the earth. And these all, having obtained a good report through faith, received not the promise: God having provided some better thing for us, that they

without us should not be made perfect apart from us. (verses 35b-40)

The second thing we learn from this statement of Jesus in which He listed suffering persecution as one of the Beatitudes is reaffirmed in another of His teachings--this one from His last conversation with the disciples prior to His arrest. "Remember the word that I said unto you, The servant is not greater than his Lord. If they have persecuted me, they will also persecute you; if they have kept my saying, they will keep yours also." (John 15:20). His message here is that we are not to take the persecution personally. We must remember that no one hates us as individuals; they hate the Christ inside us. They hated the prophets, they hated Christ, and they hate us because the light of God emanating from believers exposes the darkness of their sinfulness. They are not trying to hurt you; rather, they are trying to douse the light which shines through you! In the parable of the vineyard keepers, we learn that the messengers who came to the wicked vineyard keepers were abused and even killed, but it was not they themselves which were the object of the persecution--it was the vineyard owner whom they represented. In fact, Jesus Himself went so far as to ask Saul of Tarsus why he was persecuting Him (Christ) even though all the injuries he had inflicted were actually against the church members.

A third quote from Jesus gives us a directive on how to respond to those who inflict persecution upon us. "But I say unto you, Love your enemies, bless them that curse you, do good to them that hate you, and pray for them which despitefully use you, and persecute you." (Matthew 5:44) We all have a natural reflex of wanting to fight back at those who hurt us, but we have learned that two wrongs don't make a right so we try not to hurt those who hurt us. However, Christ takes us far beyond this level by telling us to do good to them.   Before we react to such a statement, we must remember that Jesus did just that by crying out to the Father to forgive the very ones who were crucifying Him.

Stephen, the first martyr, followed the example of the Lord by praying for the violent mob as they stoned him to death. Even more personally, we must include ourselves in the list of "bad guys" who received the love of Christ. Romans 5:10 reminds us that Christ died for us while we were still His enemies. The Apostle Paul, who had the unusual experience of being both a persecutor of the faith and then one who received persecution for his faith, echoed the words of our Lord in Romans 12:14, "Bless them which persecute you: bless, and curse not."

  I see a couple important points concerning why we are directed to pray for our persecutors. The first is that it turns our focus away from ourselves. Without an external focus, we become self-centered. Elijah presents himself as an example of how God deals with those who turn inward and weep over their persecution. When he lamented that he was the only prophet yet alive and that he should just as soon be dead as well, God soundly rebuked him and revealed to him that there were yet seven thousand others of faith who had not yielded to the oppressor's threats. The second reason that we should pray for our oppressors is that it may actually result in their conversion and, therefore, our deliverance. Paul taught us to pray for those in governmental authority so that we may lead peaceable lives. Although this verse does not specifically mention that these rulers may be oppressive, we must remember that the Roman government at the time of the New Testament was beginning to persecute the Christian Church. In Paul himself we have a splendid example of a persecutor who was converted to the faith--a conversion which very likely was at least partially the result of the prayers of those whom he persecuted.

  When I was in graduate school, I suffered severely under a professor who seemed to almost go out of his way to give me a hard time. This went on for several semesters. All the time, I was constantly praying about the situation. One day in class he mentioned something which triggered a revelation; I could see behind the professor and into the human that he really was. I caught a glimpse into the window of his life to discover that he was a man hurting from family problems at home. From that moment, I stopped praying about him and began to pray for him. Miraculously, his attitude and actions toward me took a dramatic turn for the better and our relationship experienced a total turn around. Without realizing it, I had applied this biblical principle to my problem and experienced remarkable results.

    Another point from Jesus' teachings can be applied to help us understand our relationship to persecution. In the parable of the four soils (also known as the parable of the sower), He told of some seeds which fell into some shallow soil which did not allow for the roots to grow down too deeply. He said that the plants which grew from such seeds would wither in the hot sun, and He went on to parallel these plants with Christians whose lives were not deeply rooted in Christ. "Yet hath he not root in himself, but dureth for a while: for when tribulation or persecution ariseth because of the word, by and by he is offended." (Matthew 13:21) We must develop a deep faith in Christ which does not waiver no matter what difficulties may come our way. We must be convinced as Paul was that no amount of persecution can separate us from the love of God in Christ Jesus. "Who shall separate us from the love of Christ? shall tribulation, or distress, or persecution, or famine, or nakedness, or peril, or sword?" (Romans 8:35) We must be convinced of the promise that Jesus Himself is with us just as He was when He appeared as the fourth man in the fiery furnace with Shadrach, Meshach, and Abednego. "These things I have spoken unto you, that in me ye might have peace. In the world ye shall have tribulation: but be of good cheer; I have overcome the world." (John 16:33) We must gain assurance that He personally will avenge us. "But whoso shall offend one of these little ones which believe in me, it were better for him that a millstone were hanged about his neck, and that he were drowned in the depth of the sea."

(Matthew 18:6)

    With this kind of revelation concerning our condition, we can come to the unshakable position Paul described in Romans 12:12, "Rejoicing in hope; patient in tribulation; continuing constant in prayer." In Acts 5:4, the early disciples actually rejoiced that they were counted worthy to suffer for Christ. They had apparently come to such a very mature relationship with Christ and revelation of His plan that their being identified with Christ was more important than their temporal pleasure or security. This maturity is demonstrated in the prayer they prayed after being dragged before the council, "Lord, behold their threatenings and grant unto thy servants that with all boldness they may speak thy word, by stretching forth thine hand to heal and that signs and wonders may be done by the name of thy holy Child Jesus." (Acts 4:29-30) Their prayer wasn't to stop the persecution but to extend the ministry. It is interesting to note that they called for more miracles--God's work, not theirs. Apparently because they realized that the persecution was really against Him, not them. Since these signs were promised as confirmation to the validity of the message they were preaching, the prayer that they would continue was a commitment that the disciples were going to continue their ministry of preaching and evangelism!

    A few chapters later (Acts 8:1) we read that the persecution in Jerusalem became the impetus for mission work outside the city and region. Sometimes we mistakenly see this as part of God's plan to spread the church; in reality, God's plan of expansion as set forth in Acts 1:8 was that the message would reach the ends of the earth--not because of persecution, but because of the power of the Holy Spirit. We have often been told--and I've said it myself--that the blood of the martyrs is the seed of the church. It is true that every time the enemy has tried to destroy the church, God has raised up a new army of men and women to follow Him. But the overpowering truth is that the seed of the church is the blood of Christ. The fact of the matter is that the church grows when men and women yield themselves to the anointing of the Holy Spirit, regardless of the conditions around them. In fact, it grows best under peaceful conditions--not persecution. The point I want to stress here is that the church grows in spite of, not because of, persecution.

One last point we must understand is that we must never confuse persecution and simple punishment for wrongdoing. Peter addressed the possibility of misunderstanding this point several times. (I Peter 2:20, 3:14, 3:17, 4:15, 4:16, 4:19) The implication is that some Christians could mistake their directive to disobey the ungodly laws prohibiting their faith for a blanket permit to disobey all authority. Of course, we know that human authorities--whether in the home, school, or civil arena--are established by God to keep order in our lives. It is only when they blatantly violate the God-ordained commandments and prohibit the expression of our faith and begin to persecute us for holding to our faith that we are permitted--no, commanded--to challenge their authority and place ourselves in line for their persecution.

In all these things we have one overwhelming warning accompanied with an even more overwhelming promise:

> Yea, and all that will live godly in Christ Jesus shall suffer persecution. But evil men and seducers shall wax worse and worse, deceiving and being deceived. But continue thou in the things which thou hast learned and hast been assured of, knowing of whom thou hast earned them; and that from a child thou hast known the holy scriptures, which are able to make thee wise unto salvation through faith which is in Christ Jesus. All scripture is given by inspiration of God, and is profitable for doctrine, for reproof, for correction, for instruction in righteousness; that the man of God may be perfect,

thoroughly furnished unto all good works. (I Timothy 3:12-17)

In other words: stay in the Word, and God will see you through!

We spend so much time in Ephesians six studying about putting on the armor that we seldom figure what to do with the military gear once we get it on. Notice that Paul concludes the discussion with a mandate to pray.

> Praying always with all prayer and supplication in the Spirit, and watching thereunto with all perseverance and supplication for all saints; And for me, that utterance may be given unto me, that I may open my mouth boldly, to make known the mystery of the gospel, For which I am an ambassador in bonds: that therein I may speak boldly, as I ought to speak. (Ephesians 6:18-20)

Do you see it now? One of the main purposes of spiritual warfare is to undergird the persecuted Body of Christ! We must pray for our brothers and sisters in those secret corners of the earth who cry out and have no ear but God's to hear their pleas, who weep but have no eye but God's to see their tears, who suffer but have no heart but God's to feel their pain, who stumble but have no arm but God's to uphold them, who bleed but have no hand but God's to mend their wounds. These brave souls, like the apostles, rejoice that they are counted worthy to suffer persecution for Christ. (Acts 5:41) They, like Stephen, pray for their persecutors. (Acts 7:60) They, like Paul, would scold us if we suggested that they take the easy way out to avoid their tragic fate. (Acts 21:13) BUT they hurt nonetheless! And we must help bear their burdens (Galatians 6:2) to the point that it is as if we were suffering with them (Romans 12:15).

In the letter to the church at Smyrna (Revelation 2:8-11), the Risen Lord explained why bad things happen to good people. He acknowledged the church's works and tribulations and recognized their fiscal poverty while affirming that they were actually rich in faith. In a chilling revelation, He spoke of the resistance the church has experienced from the synagogue of Satan. All His admonition to this church is prefaced by His identification of Himself as the first and last and the one who was dead but is now alive. This realization of His identity should bring comfort to the suffering saints in that it assures them that He has already faced and conquered whatever they may have to confront. Their victory was assured as was heralded in a popular Gospel song, "Because He lives, I can face tomorrow." Even though this church was destined for persecution and tribulation, they were readily assured that it was only temporary (symbolically described as ten days); even though they may have to endure all the way to death, they were promised an eternal crown of life.

YOUR PASSPORT TO THE WORLD

*Vacation
*Business
*Missions

Whether you're going to the next town or around the world, let us help you with all your travel needs.

Vacation packages
Airline tickets
Cruises
Hotels

Visit us online at
www.YTBtravel.com/Delron
or call 719-685-9999.

Every time you book travel with us, you help us with our travel to fulfill our mission to teach all nations.

CPSIA information can be obtained at www.ICGtesting.com
Printed in the USA
268319BV00006B/11/P